T0248456

Holocaust Refugees

IN

OSWEGO

FROM NAZI EUROPE TO LAKE ONTARIO

ANN CALLAGHAN ALLEN

THE
History
PRESS

Published by The History Press
Charleston, SC
www.historypress.com

First published 2024

Opposite: Edward Joseph Callaghan and Margaret Lenden Callaghan.
Author's collection.

Manufactured in the United States

ISBN 9781467155953

Library of Congress Control Number: 2023948345

One of my earliest memories is of my father bringing home the Little Golden Books as a treat for me and for my sisters. He bought them at Ahern's Store on West Bridge Street. The Little Golden Books were my introduction to a world beyond the city of Oswego. My mother was a teacher, and she read to me when I could not yet read. She then taught me to read before I even started school. I have a vivid memory of her bringing me to the Oswego Public Library when I could print my name, allowing me to have my very own library card. I was one empowered six-year-old! I dedicate this book to my father and mother, Edward Joseph and Margaret Lenden Callaghan, who taught me the awesome power of stories to expand my horizons and understanding of the world.

Contents

CONTENTS

PREFACE

In 2018, I had the occasion to visit the Dutch Resistance Museum in Amsterdam. Visitors are asked to consider what they might have done had they lived during the Nazi occupation of World War II. Would they have cooperated, collaborated or resisted? The museum's exhibits then unfold individual stories of Dutch citizens of that time who chose those very different paths and why.

That visit was very much on my mind as I researched and wrote about the response of Oswegonians to the placement of 982 Holocaust refugees in their community at the Fort Ontario Emergency Refugee Shelter during World War II.

I was born three years after the last of those refugees left the shelter, and their individual stories have since dissolved into time and history. But I grew up just four blocks from the fort on East Seventh Street. At that time, East Seventh Street led us north under a tunnel and directly into the fort. I spent lots of time there, running around with friends, watching Little League baseball games and playing kickball. To enter the fort, I passed right by what is now the Safe Haven Holocaust Refugee Shelter Museum and what was then one of the few buildings remaining from the refugees' time. It was used as an administrative building for the shelter and is now home to the museum.

Little did I know that it would be many decades before I learned the dramatic story of the singular attempt on the part of my country to rescue victims of the Holocaust during World War II—and that it happened literally blocks from where I was born and raised.

Much has been written about the voyage of the refugees to the United States, of their individual war stories and of their amazing accomplishments in the postwar era. But what about the people of the community these refugees called home from August 1944 to February 1946? How did the people of Oswego respond? Did they simply ignore those nine hundred–plus individuals whose language and cultural barriers they could not or would not try to bridge? Did they engage in vocal opposition to the presence of the refugees in their quiet community? Did they reach out in small or large ways to lend a hand to these individuals?

What would I have done had I lived during that time?

Refugee crises continue to this day. Communities are forced to respond. I hope the lessons from the Oswego experience and response will prompt us all to think more deeply about the obligations we have as humans, as citizens of the world, to our fellow man. Then one must decide, when it is time for your community to respond, what part they will play in that unfolding story.

Ann Callaghan Allen
Oswego, New York

One thousand people are very few. In a world in which millions are dying, the statistically minded might say that it's hardly worthwhile to save a mere 1,000 lives. What is one or what is 100 amongst a million? But what is one is not a statistical question if that one happens to be you. The whole fate of mankind is encompassed in a single person, and in a single person is the whole fate of mankind. [1]

—*Dorothy Thompson, introducing the radio program "Christmas in Freedom," featuring the refugees of the Fort Ontario Emergency Shelter, December 1944*

ACKNOWLEDGEMENTS

Nearly eight decades have passed since the Fort Ontario Emergency Refugee Shelter closed. In 1949, the fort became a New York State Historic Site. The memories of those who lived during that time are now largely preserved in historical records. There are Oswegonians who did experience that time in the city's history and who were graciously willing to provide first-person testimony about the community's experiences with the refugees. I thank them first and foremost for sharing their time and memories with me. They are Frances Ruggio Enwright, Chris Gagas, Elaine Gagas Cost, Margaret Greene Crisafulli, Bill Joyce Sr. and Mary Helen Crisafulli Colloca.

From the next generation, I want to thank Ron Spereno for his wonderful memories of his father and of the tailor shop; Charles "Chip" Tobey for his recollections about his grandfather Edwin Waterbury; and Keith Sylber for his help following the path the Sylber family took once they left Oswego. Thanks as well to Betsy Zaia Dorman for filling in the story of "Fort Ontario Albert" and her family's connections with the refugee families. And thank you to Florence Mahaney Farley for sharing her mother's stories of working at the fort and a great display of photographs from School No. 2.

Great appreciation is extended as well to the historians who have preserved the precious records of the Fort Ontario Emergency Refugee Center. They include Mary Kay Stone and Justin White of the Oswego County Historical Society; Paul Lear, Caroline Lamie and Marilyn Huntington of Fort Ontario; Edward Heinrichs and Rebecca Erbelding,

PhD, presenters at the 2023 Fort Ontario Conference on History and Archaeology; Rebecca Fisher, the Safe Haven Holocaust Refugee Museum's researcher who accessioned much of the museum's archival material; and Zachary Vickery, the college archivist librarian in Special Collections at State University of New York (SUNY) at Oswego's Penfield Library. A collection of video interviews with many of the refugees and the Oswegonians who lived in the city during that time are digitally preserved and available through Special Collections. These interviews proved to be a significant resource in giving a voice, literally, to this story.

When I began this project, Fort Ontario superintendent Paul Lear told me much of the information about the Oswego side of the shelter story would require a deep dive into published accounts of the time. He was certainly right about that. I could not have produced a full picture of the city and its people from that time without the amazing and valuable online resource that is fultonhistory.com. Thomas Tryniski, your contribution digitizing hundreds of local newspapers is an award-worthy effort in preserving our local and regional history. Thank you!

I have learned that when you write a book, you get so close to the subject that you assume everyone who reads your book knows all that you know. This is why editors and first readers are so important. Thank you to Banks Smither, my editor at The History Press, who applied his knowledge and professionalism to this work and practiced everlasting patience with me. Thanks also to my childhood Oswego friend Bill McGough, a gifted writer and patient editor, and to my great friend Deborah Muldoon Hole, who has never steered me wrong on a book recommendation. A note of thanks as well to George McGuire of Bond, Schoeneck and King, PLLC. George's expertise in copyright law was crucial to navigating and properly sourcing the many resources utilized to tell the story of the Oswegonians and the Fort Ontario refugees. And a very special thank-you to Paul Lear. Despite the time-consuming job of managing the fort, its staff and its programs, Paul graciously offered to be a first reader for this book. His encyclopedic knowledge of the fort's history and of the shelter history, along with his thoughtful contributions, were invaluable.

Saving the best for last, thank you to the real historian of our family, my husband, John David Allen. John has been an enthusiastic and valuable partner in this project, sharing his ideas, network, legal expertise and love for and knowledge of Oswego's storied history. This book is as much his as it is mine—and all the richer because he is a part of it.

INTRODUCTION

The war had not yet touched Oswego, New York, in the spring of 1940. Young people like Joseph Spereno were focused on high school studies and teenage social life. The *Oswego Palladium-Times* of April 8, 1940, in fact, notes that young Joe Spereno was among those attending a surprise sixteenth birthday celebration for Miss Evelyn Houghton. An account of the party that took place at the John Street home of Mr. and Mrs. Francis L. Matott was featured on page 2 of the newspaper.

Hints of the war that was overwhelming Europe—and that would soon involve the United States—hovered like a dark cloud on page 2 as well. Headlines warned about the German and British armies tangling in the waters of the Adriatic Sea and along the Norwegian coast.[2] Still, the war was far from Joe Spereno's door.

But the war was very much at young Jacob Fajnzylberg's door. A member of the French army, Fajnzylberg was among the thousands of French, British and Belgian troops who, in just a few weeks, would be forced to retreat to the beaches of Dunkirk in the face of overpowering German Panzer attacks. He participated in the Battle of Dunkirk Beach, where the British army was trapped and where one of the most dramatic rescues of the war ultimately took place. But Fajnzylberg was not among those rescued at Dunkirk. Instead, within forty-eight hours, he was picked up by the German military and sent to an internment and deportation camp, the Royallieu-Compiègne, located in the north of France, where the prisoners included French resistance fighters and Jews. He was then transferred by train from that camp to certain death at a gas chamber maintained by the Germans on the Belgium-France border. Not far from where that gas chamber was located, however, he managed to jump from a window of the train. Despite sustaining a back injury in the fall, he was able to make his way back to Paris. There, he reunited with his wife, Sarah, and their twelve-year-old son, Charles, and joined the Maquis, the French Underground, whose purpose it was to sabotage the Germans whenever and wherever possible.[3]

Joseph Spereno and Jacob Fajnzylberg, two young men separated by geography, religion, language, culture and experience, would ultimately cross paths in a most unlikely place because of the war.

On August 5, 1944, 982 refugees from the Nazi Holocaust were transported from war-torn Europe to Fort Ontario in Oswego, New York. They lived at the fort grounds until February 5, 1946. Established by order of President Franklin Roosevelt, the Fort Ontario Emergency Refugee Shelter was intended to convince American allies that the United States was serious about rescuing and providing relief to the Jews of Europe.

As it turned out, this was the only World War II shelter established in the United States to accept refugees fleeing Nazi persecution. In response, Oswego opened its door at a time when anti-Semitism was rampant in the country. It is a story that certainly resonates to this day, as the crisis of asylum seekers rages across the world.

Once safe on American soil, these Holocaust refugees and the citizens of the community that opened its doors to them gradually began to interact. The stories of the refugees and the Oswegonians, people like Jacob Fajnzylberg and Joseph Spereno, and the impact they had on each other over the course of their lives, demonstrates how individuals can be enriched when the barriers of fear and distrust dissolve.

Author Mariam Bat-Ami said that Oswego represented "all that is possible in a community, all that is open-hearted in ourselves, as long as we keep the door to our souls open."[4]

What follows is the story of the Oswegonians and the refugees who lived together in the singular open-hearted community that kept the door to its soul open.

ROOSEVELT RELENTS

Pressure had been growing on President Franklin Delano Roosevelt throughout World War II to respond to the enormous refugee crisis gripping Europe as thousands fled Nazi-occupied territory. In a well-documented series of events, Roosevelt finally decided that the United States had to do something to help the refugees of war-torn Europe. But why all the delay when reports of Nazi persecution were certainly available? Many factors were at play.

Though nationwide rallies and protests over the treatment of Jews in Germany began in the United States after the Nazis took power in 1933, newspaper coverage eventually waned, and the American public lost interest. Assisting refugees escaping from Europe or elsewhere hadn't been a priority for the U.S. government or its citizens, as conditions such as those faced in the 1930s had not occurred before. Most Americans were focused on the Great Depression and high unemployment.

In the early 1940s, Americans also had no preexisting mindset that would help them understand the Nazi program of the total annihilation of European Jews. The word *Holocaust* was unknown, and *genocide* did not become a recorded word until December 1944.[5]

The country had just emerged from the Great Depression, and memories of job loss, food shortages and economic deprivation were still sharp. Americans did not want to compete with refugees coming into the country and potentially threatening their livelihoods.

"It's a commonplace, but I think it's probably true, that during times of economic stress the best elements in our personalities are suppressed and the worst come out," said author and professor Michael Dobkowski. "Combine that with existing legislation concerning immigration quotas in place…the need for a haven for Jews, certainly after 1933, and each passing year, that need became more and more obvious, you have a situation where the pressure is on to keep people out and the need is for people to get in."[6]

"People had the concept that when the immigrants came in and took a job that this was taking a job that an unemployed American should have, and of course, [there] was very good logic and understanding to that, if there was a set number of jobs," said David Wyman, the Josiah DuBois professor of history at the University of Massachusetts, Amherst, in an interview for the Fort Ontario Refugee Project conducted on September 23, 1986. "In fact…when people come in, they are also consumers, and they provide jobs so that it would not be a lessening of the possibilities for others, but that concept never really broke through…and so the unemployment argument was a very strong one in keeping immigration down."

Another reason, said Wyman, was that a general antiforeigner feeling took hold in the 1920s and continued into the war years. Anti-Semitism had always been an issue, but it really peaked in the 1930s, resulting in an immigration policy that was very restrictive regarding Jewish refugees.

The emergence of demagogues in American society also fueled Anti-Semitism. One of the most influential and most harmful was a Catholic priest from the Detroit area, Father Charles Coughlin. He had a radio program that was carried on thirty to forty stations across the country, and after 1938, he ramped up his Anti-Semitic propaganda on the radio and in a weekly newspaper he put out.[7]

Countering Coughlin's voice, especially as pressure grew to do something about the refugees in Europe, was *New York Post* columnist Samuel Grafton. His "I'd Rather Be Right" column was syndicated by the *Post* and appeared in forty other newspapers across the country, with a combined circulation of more than four million.

Grafton was a strong proponent of U.S. government action to rescue Jews from the Holocaust. In April 1944, Grafton's column advocated for what he called "free ports" for Jewish refugees.

"A 'free port' is a small bit of land, a kind of reservation, into which foreign goods may be brought…for temporary storage…without paying customs duties," Grafton wrote. "Why couldn't we have a system of free ports for refugees fleeing the Hitler terror?…We do it for cases of beans…it should not be impossible to do it for people."

"His articles generated numerous sympathetic editorials in major newspapers and magazines and helped win public endorsements for the free ports proposal from prominent religious, civic, and labor organizations."[8]

Grafton said, "The idea, I heard in Washington, was catching on and being talked about so I kept writing columns on the subject, like throwing matches on the fire to keep it burning, and it finally did."[9]

Grafton also knew Roosevelt personally and sympathized with him about the complex political environment he was trying to navigate. "He was leading a country very different from today.…I sympathize[d] with him because he had to cut corners and compromise. He did. One of the glories of the American system is that nobody has his own way, and I like that. In this case, he did a masterly job of carrying us into this struggle against Hitler, which he knew was necessary.…In the course of that, he had to make deals with local political leaders, and he had to do things about the refugees…but he was carrying this immense apparatus along with him."[10]

While it was difficult to deny the atrocities visited by the Nazi regime on the persecuted peoples of Europe, most especially on the Jews in Nazi-occupied territory, the State Department not only resisted continual pleas to help but also deliberately obstructed efforts toward rescue that Jewish organizations in the United States were trying to launch.

In April 1943, the World Jewish Congress asked the State Department for a license to use private funds to rescue Jews in France and Romania. The Foreign Funds Control Office at the Treasury Department had authority to issue such licenses, but the State Department withheld the request and delayed action on it. Since 1940, the State Department, under the leadership of Assistant Secretary of State Breckinridge Long, had been using a variety of tactics to limit the numbers of refugees who could enter the United States as immigrants.[11]

Lawyers in the Treasury Department, the agency charged with licensing the delivery of funds, became suspicious of the handling of the request, recalled Samuel Grafton. They felt it should have been a simple license to approve. One of those lawyers, Josiah DuBois, had two friends in the State Department who told him what was happening at the department to deliberately thwart rescue efforts. DuBois then managed to collect documentation out of the State Department, which he put into an eighteen-page memorandum relating all the obstructions and malfeasance that had gone on there. DuBois titled the memorandum "Acquiescence of This

Government in the Murder of Jews." He took the memorandum to Treasury Secretary Henry Morgenthau and said, "Mr. Secretary, you must go to the President with this, and you must tell him that it's going to break, it's going to get into the press, there's going to be a terrible scandal about this if he doesn't act and take forward steps to a rescue."[12]

Morgenthau agreed, softened the language in the memorandum and went directly to Roosevelt. Finally convinced that it was indeed time to act, Roosevelt set up the War Refugee Board. The door opened a crack to the possibility of a haven for refugees within the borders of the United States.

The War Refugee Board was tasked with the "immediate rescue and relief of the Jews of Europe and other victims of enemy persecution." That was the board's first objective; the second was "the establishment of havens of temporary refuge for such victims of enemy persecution."[13]

Samuel Grafton applauded DuBois's efforts. "Here is somebody who puts something on the line out of just plain human decency," said Grafton. "The State Department was certain that Josiah DuBois was a Jew because his name was Josiah and because he was so upset on this issue. He wasn't. He was born an Episcopalian; he died an Episcopalian. He was a human being. There should have been many more of them."[14]

The advocacy of people like Samuel Grafton and Josiah DuBois helped turn the tide at the highest levels of the federal government in favor of some effort to bring refugees to the United States.

In April 1944, a public poll on a question framed to cover the proposed plan for a temporary refuge in the United States showed 70 percent approval, 23 percent disapproval and 7 percent uncertainty. On May 21, the executive director of the War Refugee Board presented to the president a memorandum proposing temporary havens in the United States. Information was included to the effect that the attorney general's office had advised that the president had legal authority to institute such a program without Congressional approval.

Although the executive director of the War Refugee Board emphasized that the number of refugees entering under such an arrangement would doubtless be small, the president appeared to be reluctant to take action, without Congressional approval, to bring unspecified numbers of refugees into the United States. Instead, he suggested that if there were a situation in which not over one thousand refugees were actually in need of a haven, he would take the necessary action and bring them to the United States, at the same time making a public statement and sending a message to Congress about what he had done.[15]

At this point, refugees were streaming into southern Italy hoping to reach the Allies, who were moving north through that country. The arrival of thousands of refugees with limited facilities for their care created a difficult problem for the army. This was the situation Roosevelt needed.

The War Refugee Board prepared a memorandum outlining the dire situation in Italy and suggested that the admission of a group of one thousand refugees to be held in a vacated army camp on the Atlantic Seaboard would save lives and relieve military officials of a burden.

On June 1, after conferring with the executive director of the War Refugee Board and the secretary of the treasury, the president said he was agreeable, favoring "Emergency Refugee Shelter" for the name of the camp, as he felt it clearly indicated the nature of the venture. The government would be unable to provide much more than shelter.[16]

Once the decision was made to welcome a contingent of refugees to the United States, the question became where to house them. A group of one thousand, though just a token considering the millions of displaced people in Europe, needed to be housed and cared for as a group in a secure location for the duration of the war. Eventually, two sites were presented to Roosevelt: Fort Ontario in Oswego, New York, and Madison Barracks in Sacketts Harbor, New York.

The original Fort Ontario (known then as the Fort of Six Nations) was built in 1755, during the French and Indian War. In 1756, it was burned by the French during the Battle of Fort Ontario, only to be rebuilt again in 1759. In 1766, the fort hosted a treaty signing between the British and Native war chief Pontiac. This treaty ended what was known as Pontiac's Rebellion, a period of conflict in the mid-eighteenth century. During the American Revolution, the fort was burned by American soldiers in 1778, only to be rebuilt by the British in 1782. In 1814, the British returned the favor by attacking and burning the now American fort during the War of 1812. It was rebuilt for the final time in 1830, though it was upgraded several times over the next century and a half.[17]

The star-shaped Fort Ontario today reflects almost 250 years of construction and evolution. The earthworks of the fort date back to 1759, and the main buildings were erected from 1842 to 1844. But the rehabilitation of the fort was abruptly canceled in 1872, marking the end of major construction. Some additions and alterations were made from the latter part of the nineteenth century to the 1940s. The failure of Congress to provide adequate funding for major improvements signaled a long period of decline for the fort, and by 1901, it was all but abandoned.

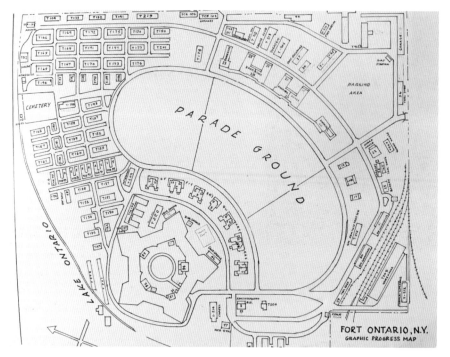

Fort Ontario map, circa 1941. *Fort Ontario Historic Site, National Archives, Maps and Places Divisions.*

Two years later, however, the fort was given new life when the government decided to expand it as part of the reorganization of the army. More than two dozen brick and wood frame buildings were constructed outside the old fort to house a larger number of troops and support services. Construction continued, and by 1941, there were approximately 125 buildings on the fort site.[18]

There has been much speculation about why Roosevelt chose Fort Ontario in Oswego. It's possible that Roosevelt's familiarity with Oswego made it the logical choice for him.

Prior to his election as president, Roosevelt visited Oswego at least five times. His first visit occurred in late September 1913, when he served as assistant secretary of the navy. The area's Congressional representative at the time was Luther Mott, a classmate and friend of Roosevelt from their days at Harvard University. Both shared a love of history. The occasion was a dedication ceremony for the Fort George Monument in Montcalm Park, which was situated close to the Mott home. The park had formerly been the location of a Native burial ground, a fort and an ice skating rink

Franklin Delano Roosevelt visits Fort Ontario in 1931 for a celebration of Governor's Day. *Fort Ontario Historic Site.*

and was being repurposed as a botanical garden for the Oswego State Teachers College.

With Roosevelt's Harvard classmate Congressman Luther Mott in Washington attending to government business, his father, Colonel John Mott, met Roosevelt when he arrived by train and served as host and escort for the visit. On September 30, Roosevelt had breakfast at the Mott home, where he worked on the dedication speech he was to deliver later that day. Before the official dedication ceremony, Mott accompanied him to the gunboat *Sandoval*, docked near the end of Market Street. The men boarded the boat, where the flag of the secretary of the navy waved, and a gunboat salute took place.

Their next stop was Fort Ontario, where the guard turned out to salute Roosevelt. Lunch and a parade through the town followed. Over one thousand people were waiting at Montcalm Park when Roosevelt arrived. The speech Roosevelt delivered that day, titled "Montcalm's Victory," is considered one of his master speeches. Before his return to Washington, Roosevelt remarked that he was greatly pleased with Oswego.

He returned in 1920, when he was a candidate for vice president, to deliver a speech at the Hotel Pontiac. In 1925, he returned to the fort's parade grounds. In 1930, Roosevelt dedicated the cornerstone for the college's new industrial arts building, and in 1931, he was once again at the fort to review the military unit stationed there during a celebration of Governor's Day. On this occasion, Eleanor Roosevelt accompanied her husband, who was now the governor of the State of New York. During this visit, Roosevelt took time to sit on a bench near the fort overlooking the lake. There, he talked about the city and the fort's great military history.

In 1944, Roosevelt, now the president of the United States and presented with two choices for the first Emergency Refugee Shelter for refugees from the Holocaust, is reported to have said, "Fort Ontario is my camp!" He chose it over Madison Barracks at Sacketts Harbor.[19]

Why Oswego?

Oswego's selection as the city that would house the country's first emergency refugee shelter made sense considering timing and the community's temperament.

The year before the refugees arrived, in June 1943, Oswego was the star of a nationwide effort sponsored by the national United Nations Committee. The city was to be featured in a government-produced film as a typical American community in a small city to demonstrate the diversity of the country.

City leaders rose to the occasion by developing a weeklong citywide celebration that brought representative war heroes of the Allied military forces to the city. "With prayer, pageantry and solemn resolve, they opened their churches, schools, factories and homes to visitors from many lands in a community-organized effort to get to know their country's Allies as they would new neighbors down the street," reported the *New York Times*.[20]

The event began with a national broadcast from a microphone set up on West First Street. Businessman Charles Goldstein, speaking to listeners on behalf of his fellow Oswegonians, pictured Oswego as a United Nations community of a sort, because, he said, people in town of different origin have become good friends by close association with each other.[21]

The city's history was a testament to Goldstein's depiction of Oswego.

Oswego had all the big immigrant groups except for the Scandinavians, according to Dr. Seward Salisbury, who taught history at the Oswego State Teachers College (now SUNY Oswego).

United Nations heroes march in the Flag Day parade during United Nations Week. *Marjory Collins, photographer, Oswego, NY, June 1943, Library of Congress, https://www.loc.gov/ item/2017857555/.*

The English came in, then the French came down from Canada, then the Germans…then the Italians…then the Polish…and we had a Jewish synagogue. It's a wonderful cross-section of the American immigrant groups. The first generation would pretty well stick together; the second generation the kids go out and become American; then the third generation the sociologists say that generation is trying to remember what their fathers tried to forget.…So Oswego is a very good illustration of the pluralistic type of society.[22]

Mayor John Scanlon leads Oswego citizens in reciting a United Nations Week pledge that was broadcast to the nation from the corner of West First and Bridge Streets. *Marjory Collins, photographer, Oswego, NY, June 1943, Library of Congress, https://www.loc.gov/item/2017857555/.*

From its earliest days, the fort itself played a role in shaping the acceptance of newcomers on the part of city residents. It was a significant part of the economic and social life of the town. Soldiers participated in local activities, and a number married into Oswego families.

Margaret Collier, a Black girl born in Oswego in 1910, wrote about her experience growing up in the city and living at Fort Ontario during Jim Crow America, saying, "I never really realized I was black until we moved South. In Oswego I cannot recall ever having heard [the N word]. Mother and Grandmother had both been born in the North. I had no way of knowing what to expect when we moved [south]."[23]

During the early part of the twentieth century, the situation for Black soldiers in the U.S. Army was deteriorating rapidly. Soon after a racially charged incident in Brownsville, Texas, ignited a national controversy for President Theodore Roosevelt, a regular army infantry battalion of three hundred Black soldiers, the Twenty-Fourth Infantry, arrived at the fort. They were the first of the legendary buffalo soldiers to be posted east of the Mississippi, and their arrival thrust Fort Ontario into the spotlight of the growing civil rights movement. According to lore, Natives used the term *buffalo soldiers* to describe Black soldiers, whose dark, curly hair resembled buffalo manes or because the soldiers fought like the fierce Great Plains buffalo.

Oswego County had been a hotbed of the abolitionist movement and active in the Underground Railroad before the Civil War. During the war, it sent thousands of men to fight on the side of the Union. After the war, Oswego's representatives in Congress were strong supporters of Reconstruction and civil rights for formerly enslaved people. Still, racial prejudice existed even in abolitionist Oswego.

When the Black troops arrived in late March 1908, there was some initial hostility, but the quiet professional pride and dignity of the soldiers, coupled with their active and beneficial involvement in the community, served to quiet any ongoing hostility.

The community benefited from their presence, as they patronized local businesses and took part in sporting events and civic activities. The infantrymen of the Twenty-Fourth were not all saints, and some committed petty and more serious crimes—but most involved disputes among soldiers and not civilians. They were isolated incidents. Oswego's police chief at that time said the men of the Twenty-Fourth were, in fact, less trouble than the white troops they'd replaced.

Secretary of War (and later president) William Howard Taft observed that once some communities gave Black troops a chance, they praised and commended them to the War Department. Oswego became one of those communities, and the soldiers remained at the fort until November 1911.[24]

Nearly three decades before the refugees arrived, Fort Ontario was the site of a field hospital for wounded soldiers of World War I. H.E. Anderson of Evanston, Illinois, recalled his time there in a letter to the *Palladium-Times*. "I have thought often since," Anderson wrote, "of the very good times we Army men enjoyed through the hospitable efforts of the people of Oswego.... Writing to you, now, may be giving me an opportunity to pass around to these old friends, and they were definitely friends, the 'Thank Yous' that so many of us leave unsaid."[25]

After the Black troops departed, the fort served as a training ground for illiterate troops. The town adapted well to the presence of these diverse groups and handled it successfully.[26]

Prior to the United States entering the war, Oswego, like most small communities throughout the country, struggled to emerge from the Great Depression. Bill Joyce remembered those days well. His parents, George and Florence, owned a bakery that was attached to their home. When the Great Depression hit, Bill's family lost their home and the bakery. They got back on their feet thanks to the strong bonds formed in a small community. Addie Joyce, a neighbor and one of the first telephone operators in Oswego, offered to sign a bank note so the Joyces could purchase another home and restart the bakery. "It was in bad shape," remembered Bill of this new home, "but at least we had a roof over our heads."

Florence's uncle Bill Mercier offered to construct a bakery area at the back of the house. And the Neal-O'Brien Lumber Company extended credit for the materials. All of them told George and Florence to pay them back when they were able.

Using two stoves, Florence began baking again. The bakery sold bread, pies and cakes and soon supplied places like Whelan's Drug Store with baked goods for its restaurant area. Bill was a high school student at the time, and Principal Ralph Faust allowed the students who had jobs in addition to their studies to schedule their two free periods at the end of the school day. Bill was able to leave school by 2:30 p.m. each day to go home to take on a shift in the family bakery alongside his mother and father.

"We worked together as a family," he recalled. "It was the best time of my life."

Even after his father was no longer able to work, Bill's mother kept the bakery going well into her seventies. The lessons learned during those days informed the rest of Bill's life. "I worked my entire life," he said. "Everyone in Oswego was brought up with a strong bond to family…and we knew we needed to work for whatever we needed."

The experience of the Joyce family was shared by many in a city emerging from a time of great economic uncertainty. Many had been out of work for a considerable length of time. Most were not educated beyond the sixth grade. Churches were ethnically based, and that separated people within the city to a certain extent. The worldview of the majority of Oswego's residents was limited by economic circumstances.

"I grew up in the First Ward," said Bill. "There were only a couple of cars in the entire ward. My picture of the whole world at that time was the First Ward. This gives you a good understanding of the city's mindset before the arrival of the refugees."[27]

The coming of the war suddenly expanded Oswego's worldview.

As the United States entered the war, the city of Oswego was transformed. Local industries adapted to the need for equipment and supplies suitable for the war effort. Bill McCarthy, who was ten years old when war was declared, witnessed the transformation of his hometown.

Before WWII, Oswego had many boiler plants. As soon as war was declared, they threw an addition onto one of the plants (Fitzgibbons Boiler Works) and it turned out two Sherman tanks a day instead of boilers.

Cyclotherm made boilers for factories. Ames Iron Works made sea-going boilers and heavy-duty boilers for the air bases. Diamond Match

Company…converted their production to make waterproof matches. The whole town converted in six months to war production.[28]

McCarthy remembered a building with a bowling alley was turned into a USO. He got his first job there, setting up pins in the alley. There was a recording studio in the upstairs area of the building, where it was possible to make a paper record and send a message home to a loved one.

He was a member of the local Boy Scout troop that picked up old newspapers, aluminum, tin cans and leftover grease, all of which was either sold or converted for the war effort. The troop earned the Eisenhower Medal for their work.[29] "Oswego," he said, "was totally unified before, during and after the war."[30]

Things on the education front were also changing in Oswego. Dr. Ralph Swetman entered his tenure as college president at the Oswego Teachers College determined to upgrade the faculty and attract top-notch scholars. He sought creative people with ideas and representatives from every part of the country.[31] At the same time, the college was grappling with the loss of students who were being called into military service, particularly those from Oswego's large industrial arts program. Swetman responded by encouraging 4-Fs and wives to enroll. He also attracted the 324th College Training Detachment of pre-flight cadets. These men came in groups of three hundred at a time to take classes at the college and flight instruction at the Volney Airport in Fulton.[32]

Swetman's new and nimble faculty would ultimately be instrumental in the successful transition of the fort refugees into American life and culture.

His counterparts in the Oswego City School District were quick to respond to the wartime effort as well. Superintendent Charles Riley and Oswego High School principal Ralph Faust were enlisted to assist and assimilate the large number of refugee children in need of education. Their involvement would be key to a successful merging of the city's students with their refugee counterparts.

IN THE EARLY WEEKS of 1944, the fort's future was uncertain, however. Business leaders were dismayed by the February 1944 announcement that the fort would be put on a standby or caretaker basis. The army's rehabilitation program for the illiterate troops at the fort, affecting some two thousand officers and men, was to be discontinued.

The Oswego Chamber of Commerce, after learning that the fort would be put on a standby basis, contacted its federal representatives, requesting their aid in any way possible in its effort to see that the fort, "with the finest facilities it has ever had in all the long period of its history," should not cease to be of service to the nation in a time of war.[33] A special committee of the chamber, with attorney Harry C. Mizen as chair, was appointed to find a way to keep the fort active. As part of this effort, the chamber published a booklet promoting the city titled *Oswego, New York, the Home of Fort Ontario*.[34] In March, Edwin Morey Waterbury, the publisher of the local *Palladium-Times* newspaper who would take a leadership role in guiding the city and its business community through the challenging times ahead, was elected for a second term as chamber president.[35]

Weeks later, the anxiety of the community about the uncertain future of the fort was finally calmed. The front-page headline of the *Oswego-Palladium Times* on June 9, 1944, announced "1,000 War Refugees Coming to Oswego." News coverage was very favorable, even though the use of the fort to house war refugees came as a complete surprise to those interested in the future of the fort. It came as a surprise to Captain Walter Land, the commander of the post since it was put on caretaker status, as well.

Though some regret was expressed that another military training program would not be placed at the fort, this was balanced by the sentiment that the fort's 150 buildings would be an ideal place for housing the refugees. "Use of Fort Ontario for this purpose is almost certain to reflect some benefit to the community," according to the news report, "and if successful it will probably be the means of using the post for other purposes in the future."

Appealing to the beneficial economic prospects of this new use for the fort, the report continued, "The immediate benefit will be to provide a new local market for milk, other dairy and farm produce which will be needed to feed the refugees."

Prior to its placement on standby status, the fort had employed some 150 civilians. The arrival of the refugees, the report stated, might also give jobs to many civilians once again.

In what would prove to be prophetic, the report further stated, "The post will also be known as the only place where European refugees, taken under Uncle Sam's protection, are being housed and sustained."[36]

When it was announced that the refugees would be coming to live at the fort, Bill Joyce recalled no one knew anything about them or what they would be like. Mary Helen Crisafulli Colloca agreed. People knew they were coming from war-torn Europe, where they had lived in fear of bombings, she recalled, but it wasn't until years later, after reading a book by Ruth Gruber about the experiences of the refugees at the hands of the Nazis, that she fully realized the extent of the trauma they had experienced.[37]

The war had already come home to Mary Helen's neighborhood in dramatic fashion. In those days, she recalled, sad news was delivered by telegram. People would dread the sight of a telegraph employee riding along on a bicycle on their streets, and they would hope the bad news was not delivered to their door. In the early months of 1942, however, bad news was delivered on her street. Charles C. Crisafulli, whose parents lived across from the Collocas, was away in the service.

At that time, recalled Mary Helen, many Oswego boys, including many siblings, were stationed on the USS *Chemung* in the Atlantic Ocean. Father Jeremiah Davern, the pastor of St. Joseph's Church, wrote to the War Department asking that siblings be split up and placed on other ships. One of those siblings was Charles Crisafulli, who was transferred to the USS *Truxton*. In February 1941, that ship ran aground in a howling gale off the coast of Newfoundland, and Crisafulli was among the 110 crew members who perished. The Charles C. Crisafulli Post 15 in Oswego is named in his honor.

Churches were filled to capacity in those years, said Mary Helen, who remembered attending a novena at St. Joseph's Church for nine consecutive Tuesdays. Two of her brothers were in the service, one in the Atlantic theater and one in the Pacific theater. "I prayed so hard that my brothers would be spared," she said. "That was where my faith really took hold."[38]

On the heels of the announcement of the establishment of an emergency refugee shelter at the fort, the *Palladium-Times*, guided by publisher Edwin M. Waterbury, worked to prepare the city's residents for the refugees' arrival. On June 10, the newspaper's continuing coverage played to the atmosphere of patriotic duty already firmly established among city residents, referring to the shelter as "a work of mercy." "The President believes it is important that the United States should share in it, not through words but through deeds. Every warm-hearted American will agree with him and approve his action."

Aware that not everyone in the city would support the establishment of the shelter, the report also attempted to allay fears of sudden uncontrolled immigration. "The plan has nothing to do with unrestricted and uncontrolled immigration. It is simply a proposal to save the lives of innocent people."[39]

The June 10 edition also included on its editorial page a boxed announcement that read: "The *Palladium-Times* will be glad to have its attention called to any misleading or untrue statements that may appear in its news, editorial or advertising columns."

The editorial that followed again appealed to the community's residents' sense of pride. "Now, Oswego, in its everyday life, will be an example of the American way of life, not just to war heroes but to the miserable men and women who have been the victims of tyrants. May the group which is coming to Fort Ontario find in this city a splendid example of democracy in action and after the war take back to their liberated homelands memories which help in building a new world on the ruins of the past."[40]

Word of the establishment of the country's first refugee shelter for victims of the Holocaust spread quickly, not only in Oswego but also throughout the entire upstate region. Community organizations, churches and schools began to speculate about how to best serve the refugee population.

Reverend John Lynch, a native Oswegonian and contributing editor for the *Catholic Sun* newspaper, applauded the selection of the fort.

> *This is not the first time that the military post, in continuous use since pre-Revolutionary days, has been privileged to be a place of mercy and healing. Towards the close of the First World War, the Fort was a large general hospital....The spaciousness of the Fort, its traditions, the location on the lake and on an international border fit it well for this work of peace.... Just what effect the project will have on the community and on this section of the state cannot be foreseen. It may be very little, or, in the course of time and events, it may be very large. Almost certainly there will be work here for the church.*[41]

Harry Mizen, writing on behalf of the chamber, publicly thanked the president for the choice of the fort.

> *On behalf of the special Fort Ontario Committee of the Oswego Chamber of Commerce, I wish to extend...our thanks for your selection of Fort Ontario for this humanitarian objective and to assure you of the deep appreciation of Oswegonians, and of our willingness at all times to cooperate with our Government in the vast problems which confront it. Fort Ontario...will continue to measure up to its worthy tradition.*[42]

The shelter announcement reverberated beyond the United States as well. Fred W. Plank Jr., a radio operator and member of the crew of the USS *Pensacola*, which had taken part in eleven naval actions during the war, wrote home to his father in Oswego. "We copied a press item the other day about the formation of the refugee camp at Fort Ontario. Jap[anese] propaganda even had a few unsavory remarks on the subject. So it would appear that you are getting to be quite notorious back home."[43]

Roosevelt's announcement that a group of some 1,000 refugees would be coming to live at the fort for the duration of the war, and the subsequent arrival of 982 refugees, left the fort and city with just weeks to prepare.

Preparations to convert Fort Ontario to a refugee camp proceeded rapidly in the early weeks of July. A large force of carpenters, electricians and plumbers were employed and on the job. Two firms contracted by the government for the work necessary were on the ground, with workmen coming to the fort from the various places where they were previously employed on government projects. At least one hundred skilled workers would be quartered in local hotels and other places. Once the work was complete, the fort would be turned over to the War Relocation Authority. Officials and others of the administrative force would occupy the dwellings along Officers Row.[44]

The July 8 edition of the *Palladium-Times* announced the selection of Joseph Smart as the director of the War Refugee Shelter.[45]

Dillon S. Myer, director of the War Relocation Authority, and the new camp director, Joseph Smart, arrived at the Fort on July 11 to inspect the work in progress. Myer and Smart were also guests of the special Fort Ontario Committee of the Oswego Chamber at a luncheon at O'Keefe's Grill that day. Harry Mizen, Mayor Joseph McCaffrey, George H. Campbell, Dr. George A. Marsden, Alfred G. Tucker, Frank McDonough and Nelson F. Stephens attended the meeting.

Myer expressed pleasure with the layout at the fort and noted he was particularly pleased with the attitude of Oswego people toward the projected camp. Though he did not have an exact date for the arrival of the refugees, he estimated that it would be no earlier than July 15 and no later than July 31.

All information concerning the departure of the refugee ship from Europe and its port of arrival was being closely guarded, explained Myer, for fear of Nazi reprisals on the high seas. All information, he informed the chamber group, would be kept secret until a few hours before the ship arrived, when, he hoped, the ban on information would be lifted so that newsmen could interview the refugees.[46]

Myer also noted during his visit that the war refugee camp at the fort would, to a considerable extent, recapture financial losses that the municipality had suffered when the military training program was discontinued. He was also emphatic in his declaration that as far as possible, all supplies needed for the conduct of the camp and the care of the refugees would be purchased from Oswego business establishments.

At the time of their arrival, the refugees, Myers said, would not be permitted to leave the fort. Later, however, after careful arrangements were made, the refugees might be permitted to visit the downtown section of the city and possibly even accept forms of local employment where there were shortages of local workers.[47]

If there was any feeling of discontent about the impending arrival of the refugees, it was not apparent in the news coverage or on the editorial page of the local newspaper. Surely, there were those citizens who were unsure of, anxious about or downright opposed to this turn of events at the fort, but opposition was not yet voiced in the public sphere.

One of the first civic undertakings in advance of the refugees' arrival was the collection of toys and other playthings that would be turned over to the War Relocation Authority for use by the children in the shelter. Church organizations, the Women's City Club, the Oswego State Teachers College faculty wives, the Oswego Home Bureau Unit and the Kiwanis and Child Care Committee all volunteered to take part. Donations were collected at the Women's City Club on West Third Street. Playthings in need of repair would be taken care of by the Kiwanis and the Oswego firemen, with the Kiwanis Club providing materials and the firemen providing the labor during their leisure hours on duty at the fire stations.[48]

While civic organizations conducted the toy drive, members of the community interested in clerical or labor jobs at the shelter were interviewed by the personnel director from the War Refugee Authority. Applicants for the positions filled in a lengthy form and were fingerprinted and photographed.[49]

By July 20, several locals were reported to already be employed at the shelter, among them J.D.O. Paradis of Fifth Avenue, who was designated a property custodian. It was also announced that the refugees were now en route from a transient refugee camp in Italy to their new temporary home at Fort Ontario on personal orders from President Roosevelt.[50]

Another local appointed to a key position with the shelter was announced on July 24. George W. Allen of West Second Street was named the superintendent of maintenance. The War Relocation Authority reiterated its goal to employ local men and women at the shelter. Plans were also announced to turn the fort over to WRA director Joseph Smart during the week ahead.[51]

Florence Bronson Mahaney was among the locals employed to work at the fort in those early days of preparation for the arrival of the refugees. Later, she worked in the fort kitchen. Her daughter, Florence Mahaney Farley, recalled that her mother developed a great respect for the refugees at the fort and that she also learned new ways of preparing food. Florence said her mother was a great cook already but learned a lot about kosher dietary laws while working in the fort kitchen, since many of the refugees were Jewish.[52]

On July 26, Secretary of the Interior Harold Ickes announced the shelter's readiness to accept the European refugees who were now due to arrive in early August. Ickes said that for the first several weeks, no one—not even close relatives—would be permitted to visit the refugees. Only authorized newsmen could visit. This was done so the WRA could get everyone organized and settled and make the necessary health and security checks.[53] The following day, Joseph Smart was the guest speaker at the Kiwanis Club's weekly luncheon at the Adams Hotel. Smart assured those gathered that no spies or saboteurs were among the refugees coming to Oswego. Most of the refugees, he said, were Yugoslavian, Polish, Austrian, Russian, German and Czech. The majority were Jewish, but there were small groups of Roman Catholic, Greek Orthodox and Protestant refugees. "These refugees for the most part have escaped from Nazi-controlled areas and have gone through a pretty close screening before they were selected to come to America," assured Smart. "Therefore, we can rest assured that the group will contain no spies or saboteurs."[54]

On August 4, the anticipated arrival of the refugees the next morning was announced with a banner headline on page 4 of the *Palladium-Times*. A special train bringing the refugees to Oswego was due to arrive in the early morning hours. In advance of the refugees' arrival, many newsmen and cameramen, including those representing the New York City dailies and *Life* magazine, began gathering in the Port City. *Life* magazine took a suite of rooms at the Pontiac Hotel for its crew. The long wait for the refugees' arrival stirred great interest among the citizens of Oswego as well. The next morning, many joined the local and national press corps along the fence that bordered Fort Ontario, despite the sweltering heat wave that had descended on the city.[55]

"Arriving here the trains were transferred to the New York Central railroad which took them across the river and brought them in on a siding at the northeasterly corner of the military reservation, directly to the rear of the Fitzgibbons Boiler Works' plant," reported the *Palladium-Times*. "Carrying suitcases, boxes, bundles, knapsacks and other containers into which their earthly possessions were crammed, the refugees in passing through a three-foot gate placed their feet on the soil of historic Fort Ontario where they will make their temporary homes, content in the knowledge that they will be secure there until the world once again assumes a normal program, if that is possible."

The newspaper reported that several hundred spectators crowded along the fence on the East Ninth Street side of the fort, where they had an excellent view of the refugees as they left the train, assisted by the scores of military police who had accompanied them from New York. There were many spectators on the roofs of nearby buildings of the Fitzgibbons plant as well.[56] Among them was machinist Harold Clark, who looked out on the survivors of Hitler's horrors and asked himself what he might possibly do to help. It would take just a matter of weeks for the answer to appear.

FRIENDS AT THE FENCE

Many people from Oswego gathered at the fort's fence to greet the refugees in those first days and weeks after their arrival. Whether they were driven by curiosity, concern or compassion, the people of the city who gathered saw for the first time and firsthand that the Nazi war atrocities they read and heard about in news accounts were very real indeed. Here in their town, gathered along the fence that rimmed Fort Ontario, was the physical human embodiment of Nazi persecution.

Mary Helen Crisafulli Colloca observed the arrival of the refugees at the fort and visited with them as they gathered along the fence. She lived just a block from the fort on Mitchell Street and asked her mother for permission to go over to the fence. "There were lots of people there, not just on the first day, but for many days," she recalled.

The refugees were pretty destitute, as Mary Helen remembered, with worn clothing and carrying paper bags for luggage. She was curious about them because they came from Europe, but she didn't recall being aware that many of them were Jewish.

Mary Helen was fourteen when the refugees arrived and was about to begin her sophomore year at Oswego High School. She particularly remembered Ernest Spitzer, who was about her age, and his sister Margareta. Ernest was quiet and reserved but intriguing to young Mary Helen. Though two of her brothers were already in the service, another brother was still living at home. They would go over to the fort fence every night after dinner. In addition to the Spitzers, they encountered young Joachim "Jackie" Bass. Mary Helen's brother taught Jackie how to identify the various denominations of American coins.[57]

Frances Ruggio Enwright did not go to the fence that first day. Her father and mother were overprotective of their seventeen-year-old daughter, the only daughter in a family that included six sons. Fran was told, in no uncertain terms, to stay away from the fort and the fence.

Fran's father, Frank Ruggio, had immigrated to the United States from Italy and was working for the railroad. He was a confident and fearless man who put in long hours to provide for his family. Her mother, Vita, a native of Bari, Italy, followed Frank to the United States five years later. Once in Oswego, Vita worked in a factory, but she was resented by some of the workers, who felt she was taking a job that should have gone to an American citizen. Fran remembered her mother's story and immediately felt a special connection to this new wave of refugees right across the street from her home. Her heart went out to them because she knew how much her mother had suffered when she first arrived in the country.

Fran watched the refugees from the porch of her home on East Ninth Street, and finally, like any typical teenager, she made her way to the fence. Her parents ultimately made peace with the idea, because they could still see her from the porch to make sure she was fine.

The fort was familiar territory for Fran and her family. On Sundays, when soldiers were stationed at the fort, the gates were opened to allow Oswego residents to come in and watch the marching and the drills. The soldiers often patronized the local bar, not far from the Ruggio family home. That was absolutely off-limits for Fran, however. With the passage of time, Fran understood why her father did not want his young, impressionable daughter fraternizing with the soldiers.

Still, Fran was eager to meet the young people her age who she could see gathered at the fence, and she had a skill that would serve her well there. At home, Fran's parents spoke Italian, so she, too, was fluent in Italian. It used to upset her when she had friends visiting and her mother would lapse into Italian when speaking to Fran. She was worried her friends would think her mother was talking about them when she did this, and she asked her mother to please speak English when her friends visited.

One of Fran's friends had given her an autograph book for her birthday, a popular gift at that time. Armed with her fluency in Italian and her new autograph book, Fran approached a group of young people at the fence. English was not working, so Fran tried Italian. "*Capiche Italiano*?" At that,

Fran saw their faces light up, and conversation, with Fran as translator, began to flow.

Fran noticed Eva Lepehne right away, because she appeared to be about Fran's age and because she looked so sad. There was good reason for that sad look, as Fran would come to learn.[58]

When she was nine years old, Eva and her parents fled Nazi Germany, where her father ran a pharmacy business. They lost their home and most of their possessions, including a dollhouse Eva cherished. Eva and her parents went to Genoa, Italy, where they ran a bakery, but Eva's mother, succumbing to the stress of the war and a heart condition, died there at the age of thirty-six. Eva was just twelve years old when she lost her mother. Shortly after, her father was forced to flee to France, where he was captured and then murdered on a train to Auschwitz. Eva was alone in Italy now, left in the care of the Kleinmans, who were family friends.

Eva spent the next four years in southern Italy. It was there her guardians applied for her passage on the USS *Henry Gibbins*, which was to take her to New York and then to the Fort Ontario Emergency Refugee Shelter. On July 18, 1944, Eva, once again alone, set sail for another foreign country.[59]

The war had affected Fran as well. Though she was still high school age, she had to drop out to help her mother at home. Four of her brothers were away in the service, but the others remained in the Ruggio home. In addition to helping her mother with the younger brothers, Fran worked as a welder at a foundry in town that had been converted for wartime production.

She managed to keep up an active social life, and that included recording her friendships with Eva and the other young people her age at the Fort. In Fran's autograph book, Eva wrote, "*Ti ricordo sempre come una cara amica*," ("I always remember you as a dear friend") and signed it "Eva Ruth Lepehne."

Invited by her new friends into the fort for a dance, Fran remembered thinking, while watching the young refugees dance, "Why, they are just like us!"

ONE OF THE TEENAGERS Fran saw at that dance might well have been Adam Munz. Born in Poland and raised in Antwerp, Belgium, Adam remembered his childhood years as happy and peaceful ones. Then Hitler and the Nazis came to power. Like thousands of other Jewish families, Adam and his father, mother and younger brother were forced to flee their home. The Munz family escaped from six different villages, each time just ahead of the Nazis, moving into France and finally Italy.

In September 1943, after Mussolini capitulated, the Italian soldiers, who had been somewhat protective of the refugees, left for their homes. Knowing the Nazi soldiers would be coming to fill the void, a group of about 1,200 packed up what was left of their belongings and began a several-day trek up the French side of the Alps through the La Madonna della Finestra Pass, more than six thousand feet high, to where the Italian side of the Alps began.

At the summit, they encountered friendly and helpful Italian carabinieri, who allowed them to stay in their barracks for the night. The next day, they descended into the valley, exhausted but alive, only to hear that the German soldiers were in the village. Nearly five hundred of that group were ultimately captured by the German SS. The rest, including the Munz family, retreated to the mountains again to hide.[60]

Taking flight once again, the family arrived in Rome, which had been liberated by the Allies in May 1944. The family members were temporarily separated. Adam was hidden at a boarding school run by Marist brothers. Adam's mother was seriously ill at the time with a thyroid condition that was impacting her breathing and overall health. While in Rome, they heard of an opportunity to apply for passage to the United States. Even though their residence in the United States would be temporary, just for the duration of the war, the Munz family applied and were accepted. By the end of July, Adam and his family were on board the troop ship *Henry Gibbins* headed for New York.[61]

The details of the past can blur together or be confused with retelling five or six decades later, but Adam Munz and his family were definitely among the 982 refugees who arrived at the Fort Ontario Emergency Refugee Shelter on August 5, 1944.

Adam remembered going to the fence where so many people from Oswego were lined up during those first days at the shelter. He was an avid ping-pong player, honing his skills whenever and wherever he could on the flight through

Adam Munz at the entrance to Fort Ontario. *Special Collections, Penfield Library, State University of New York at Oswego, Elaine Gagas Cost photographs.*

Europe. Exploring the fort and its buildings in those first days, Adam came upon the fort's recreation center. There, he found ping-pong tables and ping-pong paddles but no ping pong balls. While aboard the *Henry Gibbins*, Adam remembered befriending an American GI who gave him a silver dime embossed with a picture of Franklin Roosevelt. He kept that coin in his pocket all the way to Fort Ontario and the fence that surrounded it.[62]

The coin may have been a dime or a different coin—or even a dollar bill. The U.S. dime did not feature Franklin Roosevelt's face until 1946. But Adam did go to the fence that day with some money in his pocket. There, he met a boy from Oswego. Adam could speak a bit of English, and using that along with hand gestures, he asked the young boy if the money he had kept in his pocket all that time could buy some ping-pong balls. When the boy looked at the money Adam produced, he said yes and offered to go into the city to buy some. Adam remembered the boy then returned and tossed a bag to him over the fence containing several ping-pong balls.

He also recalled thanking the boy by telling him he was a "big ass." As soon as the words were said, Adam realized something was wrong by the expressions of the people standing with the boy by the fence. Quickly trying to recover, Adam continued to explain his expression of thanks and admiration with more words and gestures, acting out a military pilot flying over enemy territory, adding, "You know. Like this." The boy smiled then and replied, "You mean a 'big ace,'" like the heroic American pilots everyone saw in newsreels during the war. "Yes," answered Adam. "You're a big ace!" International incident averted.[63]

Lawrence Carroll was eleven years old when the refugees arrived at the fort. His "boyish curiosity" brought him to the East Tenth Street side of the fort near the Fitzgibbons plant to see the refugees firsthand. As he looked through the fence, he remembered thinking that except for wearing different clothes, they looked like everyone else he knew. Two refugee men then began to approach, motioning with a "come here" gesture. Once at the fence, Lawrence saw one was an older man who was about sixty and the other was a young man who was about sixteen. Both had ping-pong paddles in their hands. Smiling, nodding and gesturing, one made a circle with his index finger and thumb and then made a hitting gesture with the paddle. It was clear they needed ping-pong balls. Money was pushed through the fence to Lawrence with the question, "You buy?" And he answered, just to be certain, "You want us to buy ping-pong balls?" The two men shook their heads in the affirmative. When Lawrence asked, "How many?" the response was "All!"

Lawrence took this exchange to mean that he needed to secure as many ping-pong balls as he could buy with the money proffered. He agreed to try and said he would meet them again at the same place along the fence the next day.

Like every other commodity during wartime, ping-pong balls were in short supply. Lawrence tried Carson's News, Jobe's Novelties, East Side Variety and Aero Sporting Goods but was only able to buy a few ping pong balls. He reached the same spot in the fence the next day and met up with his newfound friends. He slipped the balls to them through the fence then tried to give them the change from the purchase. They refused the change, but Lawrence insisted. After some back and forth, Lawrence ended up with a bit of the change, but he prevailed in his insistence that he not keep it all.

Larry Carroll, who secured the ping-pong balls. *Special Collections, Penfield Library, State University of New York at Oswego.*

In May 2000, reflecting on that encounter, Lawrence said, "I remember thinking as they walked away that I didn't know their names and that I would probably never see them again. Over the years, I have wondered if they ever told this story to family and friends, as I have so many times. I guess I will never know the answer, just as I will never know their names."[64]

Adam Munz left Oswego at age eighteen and registered for the draft. He was sent to Fort Monmouth, New Jersey, and from there, he went to the South. He became one of the first refugees to wear the American uniform. After his stint in the service, the GI Bill of Rights enabled him to continue his education. He became an associate professor of medical psychology at Columbia University and the director of psychological services at St. Luke's Hospital in New York City, where he was an inspiration and mentor to young interns studying to become clinical psychologists.[65] Had he followed in his father's footsteps, which was the tradition in Europe, Munz would have become a butcher. Instead, he chose psychiatry, based on his desire to work with people, a result of his refugee experiences.[66]

Before leaving Oswego, Munz told his Oswego friend Elaine Gagas Cost that he aspired to be an artist and work for the Walt Disney Company.[67] He had taken up watercolor painting at the refugee shelter, tutored by fellow refugee Max Sipser, one of the shelter artists. While he never went to work with Disney, Munz did continue to pursue his interest in art, and his works were exhibited in several U.S. cities and in Canada and England.[68]

Lawrence was born in Oswego in 1933 and lived there until 1987, when he moved to Auburn, New York. He began his professional career in 1952 in the engineering department at Ames Iron Works and was then hired by Alcan Aluminum Corporation to work in their engineering department. He was ultimately appointed purchasing manager, the position from which he retired in 1987.[69]

EVA LEPEHNE CAME TO Oswego at the age of seventeen with Chaim and Julia Scholomowitz, an Austrian couple in their fifties who had befriended her after the deaths of her parents. Though she had been traumatized by the events of the war and the sudden loss of her mother and her father, Eva attended school in Oswego, advancing within a year from a sixth grader to high school graduate. Eva hoped to eventually join her grandmother in Rochester, but her grandmother died before the shelter closed. Instead, Eva joined an uncle there and continued her education. She became a licensed practical nurse and married Eric Rosenfeld, an industrial goods plant manager from Nashville, Tennessee. Eric and Eva raised three children together.[70]

Frances Ruggio Enwright continued to work in Oswego after the shelter closed. At the Taggart plant, she met Leo Enwright, a fellow Oswegonian who had returned from active duty, and they were later married. Together, they raised seven children. Widowed in her fifties and with her children grown, Fran was encouraged by a coworker at Oswego City Hall to finish her high school coursework. At fifty-eight, Fran finally received her diploma from Oswego High School. She continued to work and volunteer. When the Safe Haven Holocaust Refugee Shelter Museum opened, she returned to the fort and volunteered there as well. She often wondered, as the years went by, what happened to Eva and the other young people she befriended there.[71]

In November 2003, Liz Kahl, the museum's scheduled volunteer, was delayed, so she asked Fran to come in to greet the visitors scheduled to arrive that day. Fran agreed and brought along that autograph book she had kept with the signatures of all the young friends she made at the shelter nearly sixty years before. Once Kahl arrived, Fran showed her the autograph book, and as Liz read through the entries, she stopped suddenly, looked at Fran, pointed to Eva Lepehne's signature and told Fran that Eva and her family were the visitors they were waiting for that day.

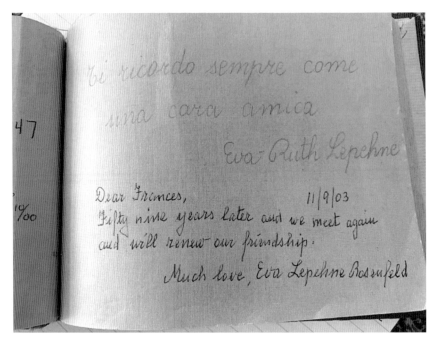

ti ricordo sempre come una cara amica

Eva Ruth Lepehne

Dear Frances,   11/9/03
Fifty nine years later and we meet again and will renew our friendship.

Much love, Eva Lepehne Rosenfeld

Eva signs Fran's autograph book once again. *Francis Enwright photograph.*

Eva Lepehne Rosenfeld (*left*) and Frances Ruggio Enwright, reunited after nearly sixty years. *Frances Enwright photograph.*

Eva's son Ken and his family had moved to Rochester, New York, not far from Oswego, and Eva wanted to see the museum that had been established at the fort. When Eva arrived, Fran approached her and told her she was the person who met her at the shelter fence and spoke Italian in the early weeks of August 1944. Fran opened the autograph book to Eva's signature. It was an emotional reunion for both women, and on that fall day in 2003, Eva signed Fran's autograph book again. They continued to correspond and get together with their respective families until Eva's death in November 2020. Even now, Fran continues to hear from Eva's family and is invited to family celebrations.[72] "I made a lifelong friend just because I took a walk along the fence to see the residents," said Fran. "It was one of the best walks I ever took."[73]

Nearly eight decades later, Fran reflected on her experience at the fence and, subsequently, with the young people she knew and interacted with at the shelter. "The propaganda in all media at the time," she said, "shaped the way people in the United States thought about refugees. Then we came face to face with these people and we learned the truth."[74]

Just shy of her ninety-seventh birthday at the time of this writing, Fran continues to engage in community service. Named the 2018 Oswego County senior citizen of the year, she is an active volunteer with the local chapter of the Red Cross, and she continues to support the work of the Safe Haven Holocaust Refugee Shelter Museum through telling the stories of her firsthand experiences with the refugees who found a haven in her hometown.

THE DOOR BEGINS TO OPEN

Oswegonians continued to gather along the fort fence throughout the first few weeks of August. Inside the fence, the refugees began to explore their new surroundings.

"Jackie" Bass, the boy Mary Helen Colloca and her brother befriended at the fence, was eleven when he arrived in Oswego. "The thing that made me comfortable more than anything else," Jackie said, "were the people… the Oswego inhabitants that came to the surrounding fence.…It was an overwhelming and emotional experience for an eleven-year-old boy…to be taken from total darkness and sirens and bombs and soldiers and all of a sudden you see people smiling at you."

"It was," he continued, "the people of Oswego crowding in welcome… who made the vital difference; kind people who passed gifts over the wire, a doll, a bicycle; people showing compassion for the refugees so pale and thin, some without shoes, others still wearing the pajama-like uniforms of the concentration camps."[75]

Jackie said, "I don't think that President Roosevelt, if he had come there, could have done a better job. I think the looks of the people, the feelings of the people and the expressions of the people of Oswego basically told it all."[76]

The adolescents among the refugees were bored and directionless in those first days, remembered Dr. Sylvain Boni, but it did not take long for friendships to develop. While the adults settled into their quarters, the teens explored the fort grounds.

The "flat rock" swim area just below where the barracks stood during the refugees' stay at Fort Ontario. *Author photograph.*

"Having no idea of American history, unable to account for the layout of the enclosure, baffled by the strange architecture, we were totally perplexed by this part of our new environment," Sylvain said. "Nonetheless, we spent a considerable amount of time playing there, looking around, and speculating on the purpose that these thick walls might have served at one time."[77]

The lakeshore was a lure for the young people as well. Boni and Rena Romano Block recall swimming on warm summer days. A hole they discovered in the fence gave them access to the beach. "We went swimming in Lake Ontario…and those of us who were confident enough to do so swam the distance to 'the rocks.'…There we rested, chatted, meditated and then swam back to shore," said Boni.[78]

"When it was warm in the summer we would sneak out and go down to the lake, and [I] would never tell my parents this," recalled Block. She also recalled her first days at the fort and the people of the city who came to the fence. "When we came to Fort Ontario with all these new experiences,

Rolf Manfred
Kuznitzki at the
shelter's refugee
barracks, 1945.
*Special Collections,
Penfield Library, State
University of New York
at Oswego.*

these new foods, new surroundings, the fence, for the first few days that really bothered most of us, until we realized that the people of Oswego, even though they were curious about us, what they wanted to do was help."[79]

"The people of Oswego, with remarkably few exceptions, received us warmly and generously," recalled Rolf Manfred Kuznitzki. "The Oswego individuals who spoke out against us were few. They were exercising their right to speak, but they were swamped by the overwhelmingly kind and openhearted reception of Oswego's population."[80]

Though his experiences with Oswegonians were generally positive, Rolf, who was fifteen when he arrived, recalled one issue that came up in the first days at the shelter.

We walked to the fence lining one of the city streets to meet the people of Oswego, and they, in turn, came to greet us. It was a friendly atmosphere filled with mutual curiosity. Many townspeople having heard of the hardships in Europe brought clothing and coins passed through the links. I remember a barber of Italian descent who slipped me a dollar, an undreamed-of prosperity since my parents and I had arrived with only a quarter. I called to a kid on a bicycle and asked him to buy a jar of mayonnaise with the newly acquired fortune, a delicacy which mother had yearned for during all the years of flight. He never returned.[81]

This one unfortunate encounter with an Oswegonian on a bicycle was countered in dramatic fashion by another. Geraldine "Geri" Desens Rossiter joined the throngs of people along the fort fence in those first few days. She, too, arrived by bicycle. "I went down on East Ninth Street where there was a fence," she remembered. "With barbed wire on top added for their protection as well as probably for ours. I don't know for sure." (In fact, the barbed wire–topped fence had encircled the fort for years before the refugees arrived. It had been installed for protection and security, since the training that took place at the fort involved the use of guns and ammunition. The fort's directors wanted to be certain nonmilitary visitors did not enter while training was underway. The presence of the fence did upset many of the refugees at first because it was reminiscent of their incarceration in European camps. But the fence was certainly not erected in anticipation of their arrival.)

Geri remembered that when the refugees spotted her on the bicycle, children came up to the fence pointing toward her and shouting excitedly, "*Bicicletta! Bicicletta!*" She had purchased the bicycle herself with money she had earned while she was still a high school student, but it was impossible for her to resist the cries of these excited children. "I saw some fellows I knew, and they stood on each other's shoulders, and we passed the bike over each other and up over the fence….What little French I did know I tried to convey to them….They could keep it until the following day and let all the children ride it."[82]

It didn't take long for Geri to take the next step to get to know the refugees behind the fence. She used to swim at the beach area below the fort fence and remembered there was an opening right opposite the place she and her friends called "big rock." She convinced her cousin Bob Garlock to join her, with both changing into old clothes. They then slipped into the fort through the opening in the fence. She said to Bob, "I know a little bit of French; I'll give you a few expressions, and if anybody asks you anything more, just walk away." Together, they moved among the crowd of refugees inside the fence, listening and observing. Geri was fascinated hearing all the different languages being spoken.

She returned regularly, sneaking in through the hole in the fence after work. Geri met and talked with several of the refugees, but she became closest with Edith Semjen. "She asked me for a cigarette, and I said, 'I don't smoke, but,' I said, 'I'll certainly get you some.' Then we struck up an acquaintance."[83]

Edith expressed surprise that Geri, an Oswego resident, was able to come inside the fence. "How did you get in?" she asked. Geri led Edith to the hole. "We always got in this way. It's right opposite big rock, our swimming area; it's a shortcut for us."

The two young women continued to walk and talk. Edith was fascinated by the bravado of the tall, gregarious, brown-haired waitress. Geri was fascinated by Edith's wide-set brown eyes, startlingly beautiful figure and thick blond hair.

Geri told Edith she knew a few of the Jewish people in Oswego, but she had never seen a refugee. "A refugee is no different from the rest of the world," Edith replied. "We're like everybody else, only maybe a little bit more tired." "I bet you went through hell," Geri surmised. "It was hell all right," responded Edith, and she began to tell her story.

Edith said her brother, Darko, was the first to disappear. He was a chemistry student at the University of Zagreb, but the Ustachi, the Yugoslav fascists, seized Darko and some 250 other students at the university. Their father, a rich lumberman with good political connections, went to find his son, first contacting the Ustachi and then the Gestapo. A few days later, Edith related, they came for her father. He was sent to Jasenovac, a concentration camp in Croatia. Christians who worked at the camp later told Edith that while he was there, her father was hit over the head. He fell down and was then buried alive.

I was a rebel; I wouldn't obey army orders, curfews, anything. To save me, my mother sent me to Split. But the Italian fascists threw me in prison.

From there they sent me to a concentration camp on one of the islands in the Adriatic. I escaped to the partisans, and I worked with them....I did whatever was needed. Then the Nazis came in a big offensive and I escaped again, to Vis, another island in the Adriatic, with my mother. The partisans brought us to Bari, and from there we came to America.

Edith laughed, "And the first day I meet you, an American—another rebel, like me."[84]

Geri was aware that despite the overwhelmingly warm welcome Oswegonians provided the refugees, there were still some in the community who voiced anti-Semitic sentiments. "I'm not condemning all the people in Oswego at all," recalled Geri. "[There] were the few I happened to listen to because I worked in a public restaurant at the time....I would listen to them say, 'Why, those Jews they have it all...the latest stoves and refrigerators and this and that.'"[85]

Unlike these few, however, Geri had visited the fort barracks and was well aware of the refugees' sparse accommodations. She said she used to get furious hearing these false rumors and would ask herself, "Should I say something?" "They [the refugees] were willing to learn, to study, to work, and as far as I'm concerned the Jewish people to me are the greatest example of if you want something, sacrifice, and work for it, and I'm afraid too many people I know want the free and easy road."[86]

Geri would continue her friendship with Edith and with Lea Hanf, another young refugee. One day in the winter, the rebel friends took a trip to Rochester, about a two hours' drive to the west, beyond the accepted range for travel. Edith arranged for the trio to spend the day in the city, visiting shops, dining out and listening to music. Geri remembered covering up the tracks they'd left in the snow for their escape and that she was able to return the women to the barracks without their absence being noticed.

Geri continued to frequent the fort shelter, attending many plays and musical shows there. She joined them when they were able to leave the fort after the quarantine period of one month was lifted. Occasionally, Geri remembered being taunted, with someone calling her "Jew-lover" or "refugee-lover." At first, Geri said, she was indignant, enraged. Later, on reflection, she realized this represented a small minority. "You know, they're [the taunters] the ones to be pitied. Anybody without human compassion who is bigoted is to be pitied."

Geri knew the refugees had suffered mightily, and she marveled at the outpouring of assistance offered to her friends at the fort. In particular, she cited the Jewish organizations throughout the country at that time that contributed to the effort. "[They] set up the schools, set up the funding, put the wheels in motion...and that's what I mean. They help [their brother]... and I wish we all would do that. Maybe if we all did it there might not ever be war. If you had that much concern for your fellow man, how could there be? I don't know; that's my opinion."[87]

Edith Semjen relocated to New York City after the shelter closed and married Bernard O. Starkman, a certified public accountant, a few years later. Using the skills she acquired in classes at the shelter, she opened, owned and operated a hair salon in Manhattan, and within a few years, she had eighteen employees working for her. It was one of the most successful beauty salons on Manhattan's Upper West Side for twenty-eight years. When she closed the salon, she donated all the equipment and supplies to the prisoners at Riker's Island, saying, "I wanted to give them a vocation in gratitude for what America and Oswego gave me."[88]

Geri Desens married John Rossiter in 1949. Together, they raised two sons.

Geri continued to correspond with Edith after the shelter closed in early 1946 and visited Edith in New York City. They reunited at the fiftieth reunion of the Fort Ontario refugees in 1994.

While the informal, individual welcomes continued at the fort fence, a more formal welcome ceremony took place the day after the refugee group arrived.

As the *Palladium-Times* reported, "The parade ground at Fort Ontario presented a unique scene Sunday afternoon when the refugees who arrived Saturday from war-torn Europe gathered in front of a platform and heard officials of the War Relocation Authority personally assure them that they will enjoy many of the privileges of the people of democratic Americas as long as they are wards of Uncle Sam."

In addition to federal officials, about one hundred townspeople attended the welcome ceremony. Joseph Smart, the shelter's new director, served as the master of ceremonies. Twenty-five-year-old Fredi Baum, a veteran of the Yugoslavian army and a fluent German speaker, translated for the refugees. Army captain Lewis Korn, who accompanied the refugees from Italy, was in attendance as well.

Rabbi Sidney Bialik of Adath Israel Temple in Oswego had a special message from the Jewish community of Oswego. "'In the name of the five million Jews in America, I greet you dear friends and extend to you our best wishes and a hearty welcome.'…Rabbi Bialik concluded with a memorial service for the millions of victims killed and massacred by the Nazis. The entire audience broke out in bitter tears, as almost every family had lost members in a tragic manner."[89]

Those first weeks brought a flurry of activity at the fort and in the town. The executive committee of the Retail Merchants Bureau met and planned to set up a canteen at the shelter to provide shoes, clothing and other necessities while the refugees were still under quarantine. Local businessman Ralph Shapiro directed the establishment of the canteen.[90]

Welcome ceremony, August 6, 1944. *Special Collections, Penfield Library, State University of New York at Oswego.*

Shapiro was a familiar face to the refugees, as he was the man who stepped onto the train when it pulled in next to the fort that first day. Shapiro managed to allay the fears of some, who again saw windowless warehouses and a fence with barbed wire, by speaking to them in Yiddish and asking for a volunteer to come with him to inspect the shelter and report back to the rest.

"I remember my father's tears (which he was not given to) when he told my mother and me how little the refugees had when they arrived in Oswego," recalled Linda Shapiro Weinstein. Even as a young child, Linda was prompted to share some of her toys, and she remembered standing by the fort fence trying to get her toys to the outstretched hands on the other side. She shared birthday parties and other special events with the refugee children at the shelter. And her parents, Ralph and Lenore, provided home hospitality to some of the refugees once the monthlong quarantine was lifted.

Linda was also told that on occasion, her father would smuggle people out of the shelter in the trunk of his car to help them avoid their limited passes for time in the outside world. A community leader, Shapiro was president of the local Red Cross chapter and would go on to serve as the mayor of Oswego from 1960 to 1966.[91]

Perhaps the most poignant message that Ralph Shapiro left for the refugees and Oswego is written on his headstone: "Separate not thyself from the community."[92]

Representatives of the Orthodox Jewry of the United States arrived during the first week to assist with the establishment of an Orthodox synagogue and kosher kitchen.[93]

Catholic services at the shelter were arranged by Reverend James Shanahan, the pastor of St. Paul's Church.

Rabbi Sidney Bialik of Temple Adath Israel. *Marjory Collins, photographer, Oswego, NY, June 1943, Library of Congress, https://www.loc.gov/item/2017857555/.*

A call also went out to local barbers, beauticians, shoe repairers and dry cleaners, whose services were needed at the shelter.[94]

Among those who responded to the call was James Scandura, the owner of Jimmie's Oak Hill Barber Shop on East Seventh Street, not far from the fort. One of Scandura's customers was Harry Lasky, the president of the Netherland Dairy. Lasky asked Scandura to come over to the shelter to help, and he personally donated a barber's chair and other equipment for Scandura to use there.[95] After putting in full days at his own shop, Scandura did just that, donating his services throughout the shelter's eighteen-month existence. He continued to count as customers several of the refugees who opted to stay in Oswego once the shelter closed. One of his customers was Branko (John) Kaufman, who operated a photography studio in the city until he relocated to California in the mid-1950s. Scandura operated the barbershop for fifty-five years before retiring in 1983. At that time, he was often cutting hair for fifth-generation customers.[96]

In a speech to the Oswego Rotary Club in mid-August, shelter director Joseph Smart remarked on the people of Oswego and their demonstration of the traditional American sympathy for the underdog. "The fence surrounding the Fort facing East Ninth Street is thronged each evening," he said, "with local citizens eager to make friends with the Europeans and make them welcome here."[97]

Expressions of friendship and support continued through the month, with gifts of dolls from delegations of girls representing the summer playground programs at Fitzhugh Park and Otis Field.[98]

Two joyful celebrations took place in those early weeks as well: the weddings of shelter residents Marianne Manya Hart-Myer to Ernest Bruer and of Margaret Frank to Paul Aufricht. Though Hart-Myer had traveled alone from Europe to the shelter, she was not alone on her wedding day, as some nine hundred of her fellow refugees, along with the entire War Relocation Administration staff at the fort, were in attendance.[99] Oswego resident Mae Kosoff Tompkins made certain the bride had a wedding ring as well, donating one for the special occasion.[100]

The wedding of Frank and Aufricht followed the Bruer wedding. Margaret Frank's attendants included Mrs. Harry Lasky of Oswego and Ruth Gruber of New York City, who had accompanied the refugees on their voyage from Italy to the United States and who continued to counsel and advocate for the refugee group throughout their stay at Fort Ontario.[101]

As shelter residents settled in and organized, local leaders formalized the support efforts on the city side. Anticipating a lifting of the quarantine period by early September, the shelter authorities solicited the formation of a committee of Oswego citizens to act in an advisory capacity to ensure effective interactions between shelter residents and city dwellers.

Attorney Harry C. Mizen was named chairman, Reverend James M. Shanahan vice-chairman and Ralph M. Faust secretary, along with members: Charles E. Riley, Robert L. Allison, Ralph Shapiro, Daniel A. Williams, Harry B. Lasky, Charles G. Goldstein, Dr. Ralph W. Swetman, Edwin M. Waterbury, Mrs. Anna S. Riley, Miss Marian Mackin, Dr. Charles Wells, James Lally, Miss Juanita Kersey, Miss Marion Mahar, L.A. Mohnkern, Miss Margaret Roach, John O'Connor, Reverend W.T. Griffith, Matthew Barclay, Hugh C. Franklin, Reverend J.J. Davern, Rabbi Sidney Bialik, Mayor Joseph McCaffrey and Mrs. Francis D. Culkin.[102]

Particularly instrumental in organizing cooperation between the city and the shelter was Harry Lasky, the president and general manager of Netherland Dairy and Warehouse and the president of Congregation Adath Israel. During the war years, he supported the war effort by storing and forwarding most of the quinine supply needed by the troops fighting in the

Pacific theater. Lasky's oldest son, Joel, remembered entering the fort on a number of occasions when his father met with government officials and shelter administrative staff to assess the needs of the refugees.[103]

The Oswego Advisory Group went to work immediately, responding to two of the chief concerns of shelter residents. The first was the need to provide formal education for the shelter's young people. The committee unanimously recommended that the public and private educational facilities of the city be made available to these children when and if desired. The second recommendation was that the refugees be allowed to leave the shelter to enter the city to shop and to visit.[104]

By the beginning of September, the door to the city of Oswego had fully opened.

The "Dowager Queens" and the Power of the Press

Brooklyn-born Ruth Gruber was just thirty-three years old and serving as a special assistant to Secretary of the Interior Harold Ickes when she was assigned to accompany the group of Holocaust refugees finally allowed into the United States in 1944. Though she was still a young woman, Gruber was uniquely qualified for the task. She was the youngest person in the world to receive a doctorate at that time. While working on her doctorate in Germany in the 1930s, Gruber witnessed Hitler's rise, and once she was back in America, she worked to spread awareness of the dangers of Nazism. As a foreign correspondent for the *New York Herald Tribune*, she was the first to fly from Siberia into the Soviet Arctic.[105]

Acutely aware that this first group of refugees would need a guiding hand on their journey from terror to a peaceful haven, Gruber went to see her boss, Harold Ickes. "Mr. Secretary, these refugees are going to be terrified—traumatized. Someone needs to fly over and hold their hand." "You're right," Ickes responded. "I'm going to send you."[106]

"Aboard the ship, Dr. Gruber assumed the only rank that commands more respect than general: that of a mother. The refugees, some of them too old to walk, actually called her 'Mother Ruth.' Fluent in German and Yiddish, she organized English lessons, cared for the seasick and taught at least one refugee her first English song—'You Are My Sunshine,'" the *Boston Globe* reported.[107]

Gruber traveled with the refugees to Fort Ontario and stayed with them during their first anxious weeks. On a short visit back to New York City, she continued to worry about how best to serve this special group. A dinner invitation from one of the city's most influential media owners provided an answer.

Mrs. Ogden Reid, "Queen Helen," as a national magazine had labeled her, was a publishing giant and owner of the *New York Herald Tribune*, the most powerful Republican newspaper in the country. Among Helen Reid's dinner guests that evening were John and Betty Cowles. He was a senior member of the Cowles publishing empire, the owner of the *Des Moines Register*, the *Minneapolis Tribune* and *Look* magazine.

Gruber recalled thinking that these publishing giants could create a climate of sympathy throughout the country, and if so, more refugees might be saved, more havens opened.

Her biggest surprise came when Helen Reid asked Ruth to relate her experiences bringing the refugees from Italy and assisting with their settlement at Fort Ontario. Ruth was describing the train ride to Oswego when Betty Bates Cowles "leapt from her chair, her eyes dancing," and declared, "Oswego is my hometown! I was born there. My mother's still there; they call her the Dowager Queen."

Betty Cowles phoned her mother, Florence Bates, telling her to open every door she could for Ruth.[108]

Florence Bates was a powerful civic leader. She managed her family's real estate dynasty. Not only was she Oswego's largest property owner and taxpayer, but she also had a history with the fort, volunteering at the fort's hospital during World War I.[109]

The next day, when Ruth presented herself at the home of Oswego's "Dowager Queen," Florence Bates was ready. Ruth remembered that "however Florence Bates worked, she helped create the climate of goodwill we needed and opened innumerable doors, as did many others, merchants, educators, lawyers, and religious leaders."[110]

One of those doors belonged to Edwin M. Waterbury, the owner and publisher of Oswego's daily newspaper, the *Palladium-Times*.

Waterbury had come to Oswego in 1922, after a distinguished career with the Corning, New York *Evening Leader*. In 1925, he succeeded in combining Oswego's competing dailies, the *Oswego Times* and the *Oswego Palladium*, into the *Oswego Palladium-Times*.[111]

His family resided on Montcalm Street, right across from the historic Montcalm Park, a location that suited Waterbury's love of history. It was that same park that President Franklin Roosevelt had visited in 1913 as assistant secretary of the navy to dedicate the Fort George Monument. Waterbury

Left: Florence Morley Bates. *Right*: Elizabeth "Betty" Bates Cowles. *Oswego County Historical Society.*

would cross paths with Roosevelt in 1929 while serving as president of the New York Associated Dailies. Roosevelt was then governor of New York State, and Waterbury presented him with a large floral arrangement from the association to mark Roosevelt's birthday.

Edwin Waterbury's grandson Charles "Chip" Tobey remembered visiting the house on Montcalm Street, where his grandfather and his second wife, Marie, raised eight children. Though the house was a grand old historic home, complete with a music room, Chip recalled that all the children were well-grounded. And they revered their father. "He was always held up by everyone in the family as a true journalist," recalled Chip. "His editorials were fair, honest and probing."

"He was also focused on preserving history," remembered Chip, "but not so much interested in taking credit for doing so."[112] Indeed, Waterbury was instrumental in the revival and strengthening of the Oswego County Historical Society, which he served as president for many years.

By the time the refugees arrived, Waterbury was an influential publisher, businessman and community leader. He was the president of the Oswego Chamber of Commerce, president of the Oswego County Historical Society

Edwin Waterbury, the president of the New York Associated Dailies (*left*), presents then Governor Franklin Roosevelt with a floral arrangement to mark the governor's birthday. *Jonathon Waterbury Genealogy, Grace A. Waterbury and Edwin M. Waterbury,* Oswego Palladium-Times, *1930.*

and a member of the newly formed Oswego Advisory Committee on the refugee shelter. Among his many civic involvements, Waterbury had also served as president of the Oswego County Health Committee, which erected a children's health camp that continues to operate today as Camp Hollis.[113]

In late August and early September 1944, however, Waterbury's leadership and expertise were focused on ensuring a successful exchange between Oswego's citizens and the shelter residents.

"Scraps of information stories about the life at the shelter are in circulation everywhere," the August 29 edition of the *Palladium*-Times reported.

> *However, some of these stories are not founded on fact or, in the telling, become slightly distorted interpretations of the policies of the shelter management.*
>
> *In order that the people of Oswego may know the true facts and be better able to understand the Shelter program, the Citizens Advisory committee has appointed a special sub-committee of rumors and stories....Stories about the Shelter will be collected by the Rumor committee, reported to the Fort Authorities, and the facts made public by the committee.*[114]

Reverend J.J. Davern, pastor of St. Joseph's Roman Catholic Church; Rabbi Sidney Bialik of Adath Israel Synagogue; Miss Marion Mahar, an instructor at State Teachers College; Reverend W.T. Griffith, pastor of Congregational Church; and Edwin M. Waterbury, the publisher of the *Oswego Palladium-Times*, were named to the committee.[115]

The *Palladium-Times*'s rumor response went to work immediately, listing current rumors circulating with the facts about those rumors. Among the rumors was that the refugees' milk was bought from one company while other concerns were not allowed on the grounds. The fact, the newspaper reported, was that "the contract for milk used in the refugee dining halls

Oswego Palladium-Times publisher Edwin Morey Waterbury in his newspaper office 1943. *Library of Congress, Prints and Photographs Division, Farm Security Administration/Office of War Information, Black and white negatives.*

was let to the lowest bidder. The families of shelter employees purchase milk for their own use from whomever they choose. Any dairy is free to serve them at all times."

There was a rumor regarding ice cream as well that said the ice cream supply in Oswego was limited because of refugee demands. In fact, the paper reported, no ice cream had been served in the refugee dining halls. At the shelter canteen, as everywhere else in the nation, supplies were limited by the rigid government quotas established for the sale of ice cream.[116]

A big step forward in limiting rumor and speculation about the shelter occurred with the lifting of the quarantine. All Oswego citizens were invited to an open house program on Sunday, September 3. The open house would not only attract visits from Oswegonians, but hundreds of family members and friends of the refugees now in the United States planned to visit the shelter as well. Such was the demand that Oswego's hotels soon filled with scores of requests. Oswego's advisory committee responded by asking city residents to consider making their spare rooms available for those who requested accommodations for two days or longer.[117]

Labor Day weekend 1944 saw the city again become the focus of regional and national attention. Hundreds arrived for the special programs conducted at the fort as the door between city and shelter opened for good. Initially, visitors had been allowed into the fort with special passes.[118]

Reunions between the war refugees and their relatives and friends took place beginning Saturday, September 2, with guests arriving by train and automobile from many parts of the country. The largest number of reunions and visitations was expected on Sunday, September 3, with hundreds of residents from Oswego and the region expected when the gates opened at 1:00 p.m.[119]

In the end, more than ten thousand visited the shelter over the long weekend.

Ruth Gruber recalled in her book *Haven* that civic leader Florence Bates and members of the Oswego Advisory Committee led throngs of mostly friendly townspeople into the barracks, where, Gruber said, "the sparse GI furnishings, the communal toilets, and showers, squashed the stories of lavish living at taxpayers' expense."[120]

Reunions, in some instances, brought together relatives who had not seen each other in forty years. Hundreds of automobiles were seen arriving then leaving the fort. Thousands inspected the remodeled barracks after seeing firsthand that the accommodations for the refugees were comfortable but modest and that none had electric stoves or refrigerators, as had been reported from time to time. The shelter residents put on a variety of music, dance and theater programs for the visitors, as well as an exhibition of pictures and sculptures that demonstrated the range of artistic talent among the group. The exhibit included pieces from the internationally acclaimed sculptor Miriam Sommerburg. She had been driven from Germany ten years before. Chased by the Nazis, she was finally able to reach a camp in the southern part of Italy, where she was selected to come to the United States. She now resided at Fort Ontario with four of her five children, where she was able once again to create and display her amazing talent.[121]

Though life in a shelter may be thought of as far from normal, as September unfolded and as the shelter residents were able to move beyond the fort and into the city of Oswego, they began to feel some sense of normalcy.

In the early weeks of its existence, the Oswego Advisory Committee had worked to cultivate a positive image of the refugees among the people of Oswego. The moving force behind this effort was *Palladium-Times* publisher Edwin Waterbury. Even before the shelter opened, Waterbury promised its officials that he would work to keep public opinion favorable. This was not a new role. The *Palladium-Times* had promoted tolerance for the Black soldiers who had trained at the fort. Waterbury was especially effective in his capacity as a member of the advisory committee's committee on rumors. Here, he heard all the malicious rumors about the refugees that had been circulating around town. After investigating these stories, he published a column in his paper, "Fiction, Fact about Refugees," to refute them before they got out of hand.[122]

The "Fiction, Fact About Refugees" column in the September 5 issue of the *Palladium-Times* took on four such rumors.

> *Fiction: Applicants for shoe stamps at the Oswego Ration Board have been refused stamps and told that the refugees come first.*

> *Fact: The shoe stamps required for the refugees are being furnished through the District Office and not through the Oswego Ration Board. The stamps are in no way "charged" to the local office or affect in any manner the allotment of stamps for civilians of Oswego and vicinity.*
>
> *Fiction: A car full of relatives of refugees was driven all the way here from California. How did these relatives get the gasoline allotment for the trip?*
>
> *Fact: Some visitors have come by car but none from so great a distance as California. One of the War Refugee Authority employees at the Fort has a car with California license plates. This has been used on the streets of Oswego and probably caused the report of the visitors coming here from California.*
>
> *Fiction: A new manufacturing plant will soon be opened in Oswego to employ only refugees.*
>
> *Fact: Residents of the shelter are not permitted to accept private employment or compete with local labor in any way.*
>
> *Fiction: Some of the refugees will soon go in business in Oswego. One woman has ordered equipment for a hair dressing parlor and will cut prices of local hairdressers.*
>
> *Fact: None of the residents of the shelter are permitted to engage in private business either at the Fort or elsewhere.*[123]

In addition to the "Fiction, Fact About Refugees" column, the "What People Say" column was a staple on the newspaper's editorial page and provided a forum for commentary, both positive and negative, about the issues of the day. The column heading "welcome[d] communication from readers on topics of interest in Oswego and vicinity. Columns of the newspaper are always open for discussions of problems of public import, but in the interest of fair play communications must be signed by the writers and except in cases of non-controversial topics the name of the contributor must be published."[124]

Waterbury understood the responsibility of the local paper to serve the interests of all Oswegonians, and that was reflected in the opinions, both positive and negative, voiced in the "What People Say" column. He also understood the power of the press to set the agenda for the community it served and its responsibility to provide fair and balanced coverage of the news.

Historian Sharon Lowenstein wrote that Waterbury estimated about 90 percent of Oswego's population supported the presence of the refugees, but he also knew that the city did not escape the anti-Semitism that permeated America in the 1930s and early 1940s. *Refugee* meant *Jew*, and early tales of rich New York kin and of able-bodied men avoiding both manual work within the camp and combat overseas rested on common anti-Semitic stereotypes.

Prejudice existed, but the community's civic leaders, educators and merchants discouraged its expression, according to Lowenstein.[125]

During much of 1944, letters critical of the refugees did not appear in the "What People Say" column, but in the summer of 1945, about a dozen critical letters were published. "Edwin Waterbury ordered an investigation and discovered they bore fictitious names," said Lowenstein. "Nevertheless, they expressed views that the rumor clinic found difficult to dispel, views that exaggerated the government's beneficence, portrayed the refugees as lazy evaders of military service, and accused them of self-aggrandizement. Such feelings tended to be greatest among people who felt excluded from the local power structure or who felt they had sacrificed the most from the war."[126]

One of the most notable events at the shelter took place in late September: the visit of First Lady Eleanor Roosevelt. She was accompanied to Oswego by Mrs. Henry Morgenthau, the wife of the secretary of the treasury. In addition to her visit with shelter residents at Fort Ontario, Mrs. Roosevelt delivered remarks at the Oswego Teachers College. She also had a conversation with Edwin Morey Waterbury, which she later discussed in her "My Day" column, syndicated in newspapers throughout the country.

> *The other day, a local newspaper publisher told us with some pride about the rumor clinic which his paper had established there.*
>
> *As he described it, the clinic works out very well. For example, when cigarettes are hard to buy in town, and someone begins to ask whether the shortage is due to the fact that they are all being bought by the refugees at Fort Ontario, this item is published in the paper and the real answer is given. The real answer, of course, is that the cigarette shortage exists almost everywhere and is not due to any local condition!*

"I think," concluded Mrs. Roosevelt, "rumor clinics in every town and village would help to break us of the habit of repeating things which we are not really sure are true."[127]

THE HOME DAIRY CAFETERIA

Opening the town to shelter residents did much to ease the integration between the Oswegonians and the refugees.

"The people of Oswego accepted these refugees with open minds and open arms and open hearts, and they saw no reason for having them confined," remembered shelter director Joseph Smart. "The first thing I urged was to let us grant leaves locally, so that the people could have the freedom to go downtown to shop and attend entertainment and search in the town and those sort of things....Merchants, of course, hoped that the refugees would be able to go downtown and spend their money; the churches wanted them to participate in local churches; schoolteachers wanted them in the schools."[128]

Groups of shelter residents began exploring the downtown shops once the quarantine was lifted, stepping into a normal world many had not experienced in years. Rolf Manfred Kuznitzki recalled those first shopping excursions into Oswego. "I remember the gate opening up and this Oklahoma land rush of people walking down the long street heading for town and assaulting the stores....Remember, this was still rationing time.... And I remember people going into the grocery store bargaining with the clerks for fruit, apples....And the clerks, utterly bewildered, never having anyone bargain with them, did not know what to do."[129]

Shelter resident S. Arthur Lehmann described his visit in a letter to the readers of the *Palladium-Times*.

You have hardly an idea what such a day, such a promenade signifies for us all. After so many years of emigration, hunted from one land, one town or village to other places, interned during long time in concentration camps, not permitted during the journey from Italy to Oswego to leave the ship or the railway train—the stay in the enormous port of New York was the first view and unforgotten impression of America—we were delighted like children to see the life of a town and of an American city.

Now, on entering Oswego's downtown, "we opened wide our eyes seeing the large road flanked by clean houses in green lawn covered with flowers....We were astonished by the traffic regulation, in green, yellow and red, not because the system is unknown to us, but because since long time we had not seen it." Upon entering a local shop, "immediately the shopkeeper and his staff help us in the choice of suits, trousers, shirts, underwear, pyjamas....We received a big parcel, said: 'Good bye,' went out and then: We were free. Free. That word sounds in our ears....Now we are in the country of real freedom and according to my opinion our hope will be realized in the march of time."[130]

Months later, shelter resident Edmund Landau remembered his first time entering downtown Oswego in a story published in the May 10, 1945 edition of the shelter's newspaper, the *Ontario Chronicle*.

Broad and clean streets, neat houses in the colonial style, shops stuffed with goods of all kinds which during so many years existed only in my fantasy. And everywhere I was received with kindness, with this spirit of hospitality and willingness to help which constitute my greatest and happiest experience since my arrival in the U.S....And when I observe my fellow residents shopping or sipping an excellent coffee in a comfortable coffee shop, I feel that they will agree that Oswego is a small but fine city.[131]

One of the most popular places to sip an excellent coffee among shelter residents was the Home Dairy Cafeteria.

Charles Gagas was a native of Kios, Turkey, who immigrated to the United States from Greece in 1913. He moved to Oswego with his wife, the former Eriketa Savas, and their five children in 1925.[132] Eriketa's uncle Peter was already living in the city, where he had owned and operated Savas' Restaurant since 1910.

From the time he came to the United States as a sixteen-year-old boy, Charles was in business for himself. He arrived in the country alone and went to Schenectady, New York, where he was employed in a restaurant. He

The Home Dairy Cafeteria. *Elaine Gagas Cost collection.*

stayed just a few days and then left to begin his own restaurant in Cohoes, New York. It was the first of dozens of restaurants he eventually opened across the state. Once a restaurant was on solid footing and successful, Charles would sell it and open another.

Charles decided to take advantage of a business opportunity in Oswego, purchasing the Bradt and Draper Market, where he operated a meat market for a time, and then he converted the building and reopened it under the name the Belmont Restaurant.[133] He subsequently leased the restaurant to the Home Dairy Cafeteria chain, but with the declaration of war in 1941, Charles had to take charge once again, as one manager—and then a second and a third—were called to active duty.

Charles's son Chris Gagas was a young teenager when he started working to help his father in the restaurant. He earned a dollar a day. "I was the richest kid in town," remembered Chris. He did well enough that his father had him start a savings account at the Oswego City Savings Bank. It was a good investment, as Chris would go on to serve as president of that bank.

The restaurant's seating area was small, so Charles built a mezzanine area to provide more seating. There was a cafeteria in the front of the restaurant and a bakery upstairs.

When the refugees first arrived at the fort, Charles drove his family over to see them. Chris remembered so many Oswegonians lining the fence by the fort. After parking the car and walking over to the fence, Chris looked through and saw crowds of people inside. He asked his father, "Where are the refugees?" He had no idea what was meant by the word *refugee*. To Chris, these were just people.

Once they were able to move out of the fort, the refugees frequently went to the Home Dairy Cafeteria, ordered coffee and sat and talked for hours. Charles Gagas did not mind them gathering and knew they could not afford much more than a cup of coffee. He did ask them to gather in the mezzanine area, however, because he had many customers coming in and out throughout the day and needed to accommodate them as well.

"My Dad had a great deal of empathy," said Chris, "and it manifested itself in his compassion for these refugees."

Charles had immigrated to the United States himself and remembered what it was like when he first entered the country. There was also a real upside to the refugees congregating at the restaurant, Chris recalled, because they were such talented artists and musicians. Chris remembered they would often break into song, entertaining everyone who happened to be in the restaurant at that point, and he said the singing was great. The Home Dairy Cafeteria became a regular meeting place for the refugees.[134]

Chris's sister, Elaine Gagas Cost, worked as a cashier at her father's restaurant. "My father was fine with having the refugees at the restaurant," she said. "He told them you are welcome here any time and offered the whole balcony [mezzanine] seating area for them."

Elaine remembered visiting the fort as well. She was in high school at the time and was often able to go back to the fort on her own to visit. "The school-age children were assimilated into the public schools, and I had made many friends among them. Sometimes, after school I would walk with them to the Fort and join them in their activities such as sing-a-longs, games, etc. They were exceptionally well-read and talented in the arts and sciences. I profited so much from knowing them."[135]

Elaine befriended a Greek mother and her three young children at the fort. She was able to converse with the mother and her children in their native language. One day, Theo, Elaine's older sister, asked to accompany her, and she befriended the family as well.

Theo Gagas with the Ihonomow children at the Fort Ontario Emergency Refugee Shelter. *Elaine Gagas Cost photograph, Special Collections, Penfield Library, State University of New York at Oswego.*

Lea Hanf (*left*) and Elaine Gagas at the Fort Ontario Emergency Refugee Shelter. *Elaine Gagas Cost photograph, Special Collections, Penfield Library, State University of New York at Oswego.*

One of the best friends Elaine made at the fort was Lea Hanf, who had come to the fort with her mother, Zieta. Lea's father had been seized in 1941 and was never heard from after that. Despite the trauma Lea experienced in Europe, Elaine remembered her as a beautiful person, a nice person who was fun to be around. Lea was in Elaine's high school class, along with the other refugees who were eager to resume their studies after so many lost years of schooling during the war. Adam Munz and Edith Weiss were special friends as well.[136]

Lea was very popular among both the young people at the shelter and her classmates at the high school. She would go on to graduate with honors from Oswego High School, and with her mother, she moved to New York City.[137]

Lea eventually rose to the position of manager in a large textile firm. She married radio executive Alexander Frank, and they were the parents of a daughter, Denise. In 1965, Lea helped organize the twentieth reunion of her Oswego High School class. Tragically, Lea and her husband died in a car accident five years later.[138]

Elaine, as of this writing almost ninety-seven, expressed regret that her friend's life ended so early. She still remembers Lea with great fondness. "She was a really special person."

OF THE MANY INTERACTIONS between the refugees and the Oswegonians, the most impactful for both was the day the doors to Oswego's schools opened to admit the young refugees.

New York Post reporter Naomi Jolles was one of the national correspondents who covered the arrival of the refugees in the early part of August. "The chance to go to school is the overwhelming desire of the children themselves," she wrote. "They shouted 'school' 'school' 'school' when I asked them what they wanted most."

Fourteen-year-old Joseph Hirt, who spoke six languages, acted as the interpreter for Jolles that day. Hirt had worked as an interpreter for an American major while in Italy. There, he raced from airfield to airfield in a uniform without insignia. "It was beautiful," he sighed. "I rode around in jeeps and had papers which said no one could molest me."

When Jolles asked him about the prospect of going to school, Hirt said, "I don't know what it would be like to go to school in America….Sometimes I think and speak like an old man. Children here [are] lucky and happy, wouldn't know what I talk about when I remember."[139]

Despite his anxiety, Hirt and the nearly two hundred refugees of school age did enter Oswego's schools.

"The best thing that happened was that the schools opened their doors to our children. And some of the children had never been to schools. Some of them…now it was 1944, some of them had left Germany in 1933 and had never been to school," remembered Ruth Gruber, their mother figure and guide into the free world. "They were so hungry for education….They brought this hunger…into the schools and changed the whole climate in the schools and in the town."

WE'RE JUST LIKE THE PILGRIMS

The unanimous support of the Oswego Advisory Committee to allow the shelter residents of school age to enter the Oswego schools, along with the cooperation of local school administrators and teachers, would prove to be one of the most impactful experiences for the refugees and the people of the town.

It had been many years since the older children had any normal school experience. Most of the younger children had never attended school.

In the early weeks of the shelter opening, the bishop of the Syracuse Diocese had designated one of the Catholic priests to look after the Catholics at the shelter and wanted the Catholic children to attend St. Paul's Academy, a parochial school in town. This helped pave the way for the acceptance of the shelter's other children to attend local elementary, senior and junior high schools.[140]

In early September, 189 children from the shelter entered Oswego's schools. The 101 boys and 88 girls ranged in age from five to twenty-one; 10 attended kindergartens at School No. 2 and St. Paul's Academy, 41 attended Oswego High School and the rest were distributed from grades one through nine at School No. 2, Fitzhugh Park School and the Campus School.[141]

The refugee students represented about 5 percent of the total enrollment in all the city schools.[142]

Dr. Charles Riley, Superintendent of the Oswego City School District, said there were no tuition arrangements and no additional expenses due to the addition of the refugee children. The State of New York required children to present themselves to public schools, and they were accepted on that basis.[143]

Virginia Dean was the principal of Fitzhugh Park School, where, she recalled, about sixty refugee students attended. Most, she said, didn't speak English, but nearly all spoke either German or Italian.

> *I could take care of the German if the need came for the Principal to enter into the picture, and I had an art teacher who could take care of the Italian....And one of the things I remember so well is how quickly those young people could pick up English....We had to put them in grades according to their ages because they had no school records....So I simply took the ages from the cards which were given me...and planned for them to enter the regular classes according to age.*[144]

Miss Dean was pleasantly surprised that the students adjusted very quickly despite the initial language barrier. She was also very happy about the good example of behavior the refugee students exhibited, their interest in their schoolwork and their willingness to work hard, which she felt was especially important for some of her American pupils to see.[145]

Not only did the refugee students succeed academically, but they also took part in other activities at the school, including assuming leadership positions as treasurer for the grade 8B homeroom and as president of the grade 7B homeroom.[146]

"All over the world, I think," she concluded, "we would have a happier world today if there was greater understanding of how people feel and think and do in their own countries."[147] Her Fitzhugh Park students certainly gained an appreciation for their refugee classmates, electing Joseph Langnas president of Paul Alfred's grade 7B homeroom and Silvain Boni class vice-president.

Alfred admitted that the election of not one but two of the refugee students in his homeroom not only surprised him but also pleased him. The election, said Alfred, was done by secret ballot, and there was no politicking, no speeches. These boys, recalled Alfred, were of the finest he had ever encountered, and he had then been teaching in the school system for more than twenty years.[148]

The Langnas family had spent years fleeing the Nazi advance in Europe, first leaving their home country of Austria in 1938. They fled to Italy, but by 1943, with German troops occupying northern Italy and rounding up

Jews to be placed into concentration camps, the family, aided by sympathetic Italians, moved to Rome. Liberated by Allied troops in 1944, they were given the opportunity to come to the Emergency Refugee Shelter at Fort Ontario in Oswego.[149]

Ruth Gruber recalled Joseph's election at Fitzhugh Park School and that, in later years, his mother remarked to her, "In Vienna, Joe couldn't even go to school. In America, he's President!"[150]

The Langnas family settled in the Detroit area after the shelter closed. Joseph became a physician and teacher of pathology at Botsford Hospital outside Detroit. "Oswego," he said, "was one of those experiences by which we measure our lives."[151]

Sylvain Boni's father, Jacques, not only saved the lives of his wife and three sons, but he also saved the lives of one hundred other Jews fleeing Bulgaria during the war. He purchased a boat with the last of his money and hired a captain to take them on the four-hour voyage from Albania to Italy. But when the Nazis came on board while the boat was still in the harbor, they all hid below the deck. Once the Nazis left, the captain weighed anchor, got drunk and was never seen again. The group drifted for days until the ship sprang a leak. The boat was half submerged when British soldiers sighted them and towed them to Brindisi. Sylvain's father died of a heart attack soon after their rescue. His mother traveled with her three sons to safety at Fort Ontario in Oswego.[152]

Sylvain, his mother and brothers eventually settled in Philadelphia. Sylvain earned his doctorate in philosophy and went on to teach the philosophy of religion to gifted and talented students at Central High School.

On a return trip from Canada years later, Sylvain and his wife took a detour to Oswego. He had not been there since 1946. One of their stops was to see the forbidden swimming area below the fort barracks. "When I saw that jetty that had posed such a challenge to us as children, I thought that it was not much of a distance after all."[153]

Dr. Harold Alford supervised the Campus School at the State Teachers College, where of the approximately two hundred students enrolled there, twenty-six were from the refugee shelter.

At first, Alford said, the American children tended to gather on one side of the playground and the refugee children on the other, but after two or three months, he recalled, that all disappeared. And toward the end of the year, it was not noticeable at all.

He agreed that language was an adjustment at first, but it did not take long for the new students to adapt. "Many…were able to speak two, three or four languages and a great many of our youngsters in the…school [were] from the rural area.…They were a little surprised and bewildered that these boys and girls could speak so many languages." Alford related:

> *One day in the shop, one of the refugee children came up and wanted to know what language these American boys and girls were speaking. They understood French, German, and Italian but…not this language. On investigation we found that the…American* [students] *were speaking pig Latin to show* [their new classmates] *they too could speak* [a language] *other than English. That was one of the first friendly interactions between the two groups. It wasn't long then before you could defy anyone to go into a room and pick out the children from the shelter. You just simply couldn't pick them out.*[154]

In response to a question about how well the refugee children took to the American language, including American slang as well as the more formal language, Alford responded, "They did very well indeed, including with pig Latin!"[155]

Eric Brunger was a seventh-grade teacher and vice-principal at the Campus School. He remembered how the refugee students challenged his local students to think more broadly. As an example, during a class discussion about local school systems and how they work, he asked them to define a school. The local students defined a school as a building with teachers and children and books. But Vladimir Lang, who had earlier been elected chairman of the class by his classmates, waved his hand to interject. While Brunger's American students insisted that you couldn't have a school without books, Vladimir explained that in Italy, all they had were some old newspapers but that they engaged in schooling just the same. It then became clear to the Americans, said Brunger, that all you really needed for education to take place "was someone to lead and someone to be there."[156]

David Furman was in the sixth grade at Campus School in the fall of 1944. He remembered the arrival of the refugee students. "One day our classroom door opened and in walked the principal and eight refugee children. I looked at each and was amazed. They looked just like us, although most looked older than we did.…Then we stood, one by one, and introduced ourselves to them.…It didn't take long to assimilate them into our class and accept them as classmates and friends. It also didn't take long for them to feel a part of us."[157]

Typical American boys, you'd think, looking at Ignace, left, of Belgium and Yugoslavian Laddie, right. Laddie tells about another kind of school with torn newspapers for textbooks

Ignace (*left*) of Belgium and Laddie (*right*) of Yugoslavia, along with another classmate, talk about what defines a school. *Lilly Joss photograph,* The Fourth R, The Woman's Home Companion, *July 1945.*

Furman remembered the influence of the refugee students on their outdoor activities. Prior to their arrival, softball was the sport of choice on the playground. With the arrival of the refugee students, the American students were introduced to soccer. "We opted to try this new sport and our new friends were good teachers," said Furman. "But we Americans suffered physically since our 'teachers' showed no mercy during each game."[158]

As the school year unfolded, Furman's class, he said, became "the melting pot." "Through the academics, the socials, and the physical activities, including industrial arts and physical education, their scars were healing rapidly, and they were also rapidly becoming Americanized. Our class became very close."[159]

Walter Greenberg attended the Campus School and was initially placed in the fifth grade but then moved to the seventh. He was born in northern Italy. His father came from Austria and his mother from Yugoslavia. When

Walter Greenberg (*standing fourth from left*) and his fifth-grade classmates at the Campus School. *Special Collections, Penfield Library, State University of New York at Oswego.*

Austrian Jews were being persecuted, they fled into northern Italy, and Walter's father smuggled them at night into Yugoslavia, thinking it would be better for them there. He was caught, put in jail and then released, but he was told that it wasn't safe for him anymore and that his family should leave. Walter's only formal education was a few months in kindergarten.

The family lived in a concentration camp in North Africa, and from there, they were returned to Italy. After months moving from place to place to evade the Nazis, they met up with American soldiers in trucks, who took them to Rome. From there, they were selected to join the 982 refugees bound for the United States and Fort Ontario.

> *The children in the school received us well. There was an occasion, when we left the camp in the beginning, kids would make snowballs out of ice and throw them, but I think no more than kids would over here. I know that my teachers were very kind to us, and I was sick once, I had the mumps in the camp, and my teacher came and she brought me a present and inquired how I felt, and she talked to my parents....She was a lady that wasn't married and was living with her parents, and we were invited to their home, and I remember they served me tomato juice. It was the first time I tasted American tomato juice, or any tomato juice. My parents were served probably liquor or beer, and we spent a lovely afternoon there and it was an unbelievable experience for my parents and for me, because to be invited by—she represented, as a teacher, not only represented Americans, but she represented authority because a teacher, to my parents, was a teacher, she commanded respect, and it was a nice experience. Her name was Miss Sullivan....I think we hungered so much to learn about America, and I think that the teachers were able to satisfy this hunger to learn about American history and the four freedoms, and the Civil War. It was just a wonderful experience, and it was something to really dig one's feet into and learn as much as possible.*[160]

The elementary school closest to the fort was School No. 2, encompassing students between kindergarten and the third grade. It was also the school that absorbed the greatest number of refugee children. Susie Donovan, the principal, said about 50 percent of the students there were refugees but that they entered school life "just like our own. In fact, you couldn't tell one from the other if you were to come in unless they were pointed out."[161]

Hedy Gaon remembers her second-grade teacher, Miss Laura Gallagher, at School No. 2: "I revered my teachers, and I wanted them to like me.

First-grade students in their classroom at School No. 2, January 29, 1945. *Special Collections, Penfield Library, State University of New York at Oswego.*

When I was eight years old, I invited my…teacher, Miss Gallagher, to come to my birthday party. I was honored and proud to show off my teacher to the people at the camp. Miss Gallagher brought me two books. I still have and cherish those books."

New York Post reporter Naomi Jolles, who was among the members of the national press corps covering the arrival of the refugees in August 1944, returned to Oswego toward the end of the school year to follow up with the young people of the shelter. She was especially interested in how they had fared in the local schools. "Reading, 'riting and 'rithmatic may have been good enough for the days when 'going west' meant Ohio," she wrote. "But the three Rs aren't enough today. There's a big new lesson to be learned called how to live with your neighbors in an air-age world. In Oswego, New York, a generation of youngsters who never looked beyond Main Street before are learning the new lesson smartly, thanks to the fourth R. Refugee is the fourth R for them—embedded in the daily companionship of one hundred eighty-one children from a dozen different countries of Europe."

As the school year ended, Jolles found that the daily companionship of the refugee children was "as vitalizing as plasma." She recalled the

Birthday party at Fort Ontario with a teacher from School No. 2. *Florence Mahaney Farley, from a photograph donated by Peter Newman.*

Oswego children began school not quite knowing what to expect from their new classmates.

> *Then, just before Thanksgiving, the situation cleared up. A class was discussing the Pilgrims and one Austrian boy asked who whey were.*
>
> *"They were people who came here to find freedom of religion," he was told.*
>
> *"Oh, then," he exclaimed, "we're just like the Pilgrims!"*
>
> *That set the Oswego youngsters to thinking. If Karl was like a Pilgrim, that would make the Pilgrims our first refugees. Everyone likes the Pilgrims, so what's wrong with the refugees?*
>
> *The answer was obvious.*[162]

Preparation for Life

Oswego High School principal Ralph Faust embraced the integration of the refugees with his high school students. He "felt this was a great unique experiment in American history and he wanted all his students in Oswego to benefit from this new group coming in," recalled Ruth Gruber about the opening of Oswego's schools to the young refugees.[163]

Ralph Faust graduated from Syracuse University, which he had attended on a full scholarship. Initially, he studied business but switched to education because of his love of history and children. In 1926, he accepted a job teaching civics at Oswego High School.

Faust proved himself to be a dedicated educator, taking summer courses early in his teaching career to discover new trends in education. He brought the then-new idea of a "junior high" program to Oswego. In 1929, he was appointed principal of Kingsford Park School, where he created the school district's first junior high, separating the building into a grade K–6 and 7–9 structure. Ten years later, he was named principal of Oswego High School, where he instituted other new programs, including the foreign exchange student program and the student council.

With what spare time he had, Ralph Faust dedicated himself to exploring the roots of Oswego County and published several local histories. In addition, he was an active community leader, serving on the Oswego County Historical Society and the boards of the Oswego County Savings Bank and the Riverside Cemetery. He was, said his wife, Dorothy, "a caring, sincere man that kept every commitment he made."[164]

Ralph Faust, principal, Oswego High School. *Paradox*, 1945. *Oswego High School.*

In August 1944, Faust cut his summer vacation short to meet with the high school–eligible young people at the fort, bringing along the school's guidance counselor, Harold Bennett, to assist. "I was invited to meet them in one of the barrack buildings at the Fort and when I was introduced to them, they all stood up in a body and clicked their heels and bowed from the waist. That was my first impression. I was quite overcome. I thought, 'Oh, boy! That won't last.'"[165] Faust was wrong. Not only did their respect for him continue during their time at the high school, but many kept up correspondence with him into their adult years.

"Most of [the students] had been out of school for three, four, five, six years and they were eager to get back," recalled Faust, "but I had to figure out…how much…math and science they'd had and what their command of English was.…Then I scheduled them."[166]

Steffi Steinberg assisted Faust as a translator for the individual interviews.

"I hadn't gone to school in six years. It had never occurred to me that I would ever go to school again.…I had a couple of girlfriends and we all decided, despite the fact that we were a couple years older than high school age, we [would] accept the principal's invitation.…We entered the high school and he must have had a hell of a job trying to integrate us into this high school…but he did."[167]

The day before school started, Faust brought the refugee students to the school for a tour so they would be familiar with the building and where to go for their classes. When the tour was on the lower floor, where the shop program was located, Faust heard the students murmuring among themselves that the facilities were "magnifique."

He noted they had difficulty with English and used a dictionary a lot of the time. Still, they were eager to go back to school, and Faust felt they did a lot to motivate his teachers to go out of their way to assist.[168]

Though many of the refugee students spoke several languages, English, Faust knew, would be a struggle for them, particularly for those navigating the high school curriculum. To ease their transition, volunteer teachers from the city schools and the college went to the shelter to conduct English classes for the refugee children to prepare them for the regular school sessions.[169]

Marion Mahar of the teachers' college directed the impromptu school designed to help not only the refugees but their teachers as well. City schoolteachers who volunteered included Mary McCann Murphy, Grace McKenna, Mary Stoke and Genevieve Skinner, along with Irene Eisele, Marion Bennett, Margaret Roach, Jeanne Morris Kowalski, Betty Burden and Elizabeth Swetman from the teachers' college.[170]

Margaret Greene Crisafulli was a student at Oswego High School whose memories of that time are still fresh at the time of this writing. The school she attended is now a condominium complex, and Margaret lives in what was once her old study hall. Her principal, Ralph Faust, and his wife, Dorothy, retired to the complex as well. Margaret especially recalled Ernest and Margareta Spitzer. Margareta was her classmate. "Those students had tremendous respect for their teachers," she recalled.

After the refugees had been in school for a time, *Life* magazine returned for a story on how they were doing after being integrated with the local students. Margaret was chosen to join the refugee students at the Pontiac Hotel, where their photographs were to be taken and their interviews to take place. It was an exciting event, she recalled, but then she never saw coverage of the event in the magazine. She was disappointed, because she had great respect for the refugee students who had to overcome so much to restart their education.[171]

Despite the support of Faust, his staff and many of the students, there were isolated incidents where discrimination raised its ugly head. Scholar Debra Cunningham wrote about one such incident in her master's thesis on the influence of Ralph Faust. "On the first official day of school, the President of the Student Body refused to do a welcoming speech for the enrolling refugee students, stating that the town did not ask them to Oswego, nor to enter the schools.…Faust…was accepting of the situation and welcomed them himself. He felt the boy was stating what he believed and was standing by it, and regardless of what Faust thought, he allowed the boy his personal…beliefs."[172]

Not all the refugees embraced high school. Edith Semjen, Geri Rossiter's rebel friend, was caught smoking in the corridor just two days into the school year, and Faust asked her to leave. Dubbed "the Blonde Bombshell" by Faust, Semjen found her true calling in the beauty culture program that was later established at the shelter.

At first, some of the Oswego students viewed the refugees as "grinds" for always going to the library and studying, as related by Ruth Gruber in a conversation she had at the time with another student. "An American

Refugee students in class at Oswego High School. *First row, from left to right*: Nelly Bokros, Edith Weiss, David Hendl and Steffi Steinberg. *Second row, from left to right*: Paul Bokros, Lea Hanf and Ivo Lederer. *Third row, from left to right*: Herrmann Kremer, Ernst Spitzer and Miriam Weinstein. *Fourth row, near window*: Lilly Bronner. *Back row, near window*: Paul Arnstein. *Safe Haven Holocaust Refugee Shelter Museum.*

senior watched the refugee students head for the [Oswego Public Library]. At first, a lot of us laughed at them for being grinds," he told me. "It made you feel small, but then you felt, if they can do it, when they came here knowing so little English, we can do it too. I guess I'll be taking myself over to the library."[173]

Some students also became jealous when a favorite teacher, Mary DiBlasi, who spoke Italian and taught art at Fitzhugh Park School, would give directions in both languages to her students. Not only did the Oswego students start hitting the books more, but they also began frequenting the Oswego Public Library, where the librarian was amazed to suddenly find a run on language dictionaries. Understanding what Miss DiBlasi was saying in Italian was now a matter of pride.[174]

As September unfolded, the refugee students' lives took on a routine, and they gradually integrated with their American classmates. "At first there was little fraternization with the local kids," remembered Rolf Manfred Kuznitzki.

> *They were not unfriendly, just belonged to another world. Later, some friendships developed. One of us had a local "steady" girlfriend. I was invited to parties at various girls' homes. Contrary to reports heard later*

there never, to my best knowledge, existed animosity toward us, only the natural alienation felt by newcomers.

Mr. Faust was an extraordinary man with a capacity for kindness and devotion, which I now realize to be rare and precious traits. The OHS crowd did well.

Much of the credit goes to a group of outstanding teachers and especially Gladys Baker and Frieda Schuelke who encouraged me, gave me confidence and the drive for learning....These two heroines of my life, and many other teachers (Agnes O'Brien, Miss [Cassie] Marsh, Mr. [Robert] Augustine and Mr. [Orla] Loper) truly represent[ed] The Best of their profession....What I learned in those classes forms the foundation of all I know....The visit to the Oswego bank, the lessons on labor unions and American politics planted seeds, which still grow. The math taught by the red-haired Miss O'Brien and the physics and chemistry principles taught by Mr. Augustine and Mr. Loper were incorporated in the development of missiles and the operation of many electric utilities.

The war ended in 1945 and as the second winter in camp approached the feeling of impending change was everywhere. The...semester was to be my last at OHS and I hurried to complete the graduation requirements. I needed a few credits and took advanced exams in language and so was able to finish in December [1945]. The camp was dissolved shortly thereafter, but I returned to Oswego in June to collect the diploma.[175]

Rolf Manfred Kuznitzki graduated from the University of Toledo in 1949 and then went on for advanced studies at Ohio State University. He was first employed by Allied Chemical and later worked at Aerojet Corporation in Sacramento, California, where he became director of research. There, he was instrumental in the development of the Polaris and other missile systems.[176]

In the latter part of his career, he traveled around the world, teaching the uses of energy for peace.[177]

Rolf visited Oswego on several occasions. He remembered his first visit sometime in the 1970s to consult on a research project supporting Niagara Mohawk (now National Grid) in its quest to reduce its dependency on oil fuel.

I rented a red convertible in Syracuse and drove into town on a warm spring day, lowered the top, found a radio station playing '40s music and drove down Bridge Street with a wide grin. I stayed at a new motel on the river, and the familiar sound of the foghorn lulled me to sleep.

On subsequent visits, business and pleasure, I visited Ralph Faust… and we became good friends. We stayed in his apartment in the high school building which had been converted into condominiums and slept in what had been my homeroom.[178]

The annual oratorical contest sponsored by the American Legion also demonstrated Faust's willingness to support the refugee students at the high school. Twelve students from Oswego High School entered the local contest, including shelter residents Eddy Levitch and Kostia Zabotin. The speakers were judged on their poise and personality, accuracy and effectiveness and on emotional appeal.[179]

Eddy Levitich's family began their arduous wartime journey in Belgrade, Yugoslavia, in 1941. It involved nearly twenty relocations, including a lengthy stay in an Italian internment camp for Yugoslavian Jews, before the family ultimately reached safe harbor in New York in 1944.[180]

Levitch remembers himself as "a young man in a hurry," taking extra courses to accelerate his graduation. "I annoyed Mr. Faust so much that he stopped in the corridor one day to ask, 'What's the hurry?' My answer was simple: to make up for the four years I had lost in the war. I never heard from him on the subject again!"[181]

Levitch enjoyed public speaking and delivered his speech on "The Influence of the Constitution on the New Immigrant." He was elated to receive honorable mention in the contest.[182]

Kostia was born to a Jewish mother and Russian Orthodox Christian father in Karlskuhe, Germany, where he was baptized as a Catholic. He was among the few Christian refugees at the shelter.[183] "His father, Vladimir, a noted abstractionist painter, had found himself in disfavor with the Nazis on two counts," noted author and historian Sharon Lowenstein. "He was Russian and had a Jewish wife."[184] The family eventually fled to Rome, and from there, they were selected to come to the United States and the emergency shelter at Fort Ontario.

Kostia's speech was titled "The American Constitution as Seen by a European," and he won first prize. Paul Joseph Lehon of Fulton High School was awarded second prize.

Ordinarily, the first-prize winner went on to represent the county in regional competition, but the story in the *Palladium-Times* announced, "There is a possibility that Lehon will be sent as Oswego county's delegate. This is

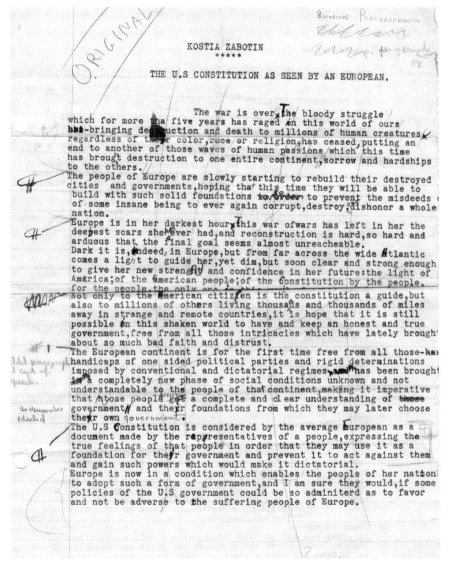

Original draft of Kostia Zabotin's prize-winning speech. *Special Collections, Penfield Library, State University of New York at Oswego.*

due to the uncertainty of the young refugee student's future residence, now that the government is processing the…refugees at Fort Ontario for legal entrance to the United States under the immigration quota."[185]

Ruth Gruber recalled that "Kostia…entered the American Legion public-speaking contest…and won first prize. The American Legion was not about to give him the award; he was not a citizen. But Ralph Faust 'raised hell,' he told me, in describing the incident, and Kostia walked away with the award."[186]

Kostia Zabotin left Oswego in early 1946 and went to New York City, where he began a career with Air France. In 1950, he was drafted in the Korean War. After an already difficult life due to World War II, Zabotin declared himself a conscientious objector and was sent to Army Medical School in Texas. There, he was used as an army interpreter for two years, because he spoke six languages. After his service, he resumed his career with Air France, retiring in the early 1990s to spend time on his farm in Corsica. He returned to Oswego in May 1993 to meet with the committee discussing plans for a museum to commemorate the refugee experience.[187]

FAUST SUPPORTED THE REFUGEE students in other significant ways.

> *He contacted the State Education Board in Albany…to get permission for* [the refugee students] *to take various regents exams in several languages…*[so they] *would have enough points to be eligible for diplomas. He got the exams administered by the local teachers with some knowledge of the languages.…Anthony Murabito recalls proctoring the Italian regents with lots of sign language to make himself understood. The students' language skills he recall*[ed] *were better than his.*[188]

With Faust's support, six shelter residents received their high school diplomas at the June 1945 graduation ceremony. Others followed, graduating with the class of 1946.

Faust's advocacy was mirrored by many of the teachers on his high school staff. Among those remembered fondly by the refugees, years after they left Oswego, were Thomas Crabtree, Francis T. Riley, Miss Jessie Wood, Miss Elizabeth Riley, Miss Gladys Baker and Miss Jane Powers.

History teacher and historian Francis T. Riley remembered the first time he saw the refugees walking down Bridge Street and how he marveled at the way they "grasped the full meaning of American freedom that they had not known in Europe," being able to move and converse freely about the stores and with the people of Oswego. And, he said, the high school teachers were astounded at how quickly the refugee students mastered the language and the history of their new home.[189]

Riley wrote in Steffi Steinberg's yearbook in June 1945, "When we look back on the many happy exchanges we had in and out of class, I feel sure that we have all benefited greatly from having known each other."[190]

Several of the young men at the high school were greatly influenced by industrial arts teacher Thomas Crabtree. "My woodworking teacher, Mr. Crabtree, was my role model," said Eddy Levitch. "He was always well-dressed, with a starched white shirt, sleeves rolled up to his elbows, and a clean apron; *immaculate* is perhaps a better word to describe him. I remember his lectures well. Among other things he predicted a building boom. He inspired us to learn."[191]

Ruth Gruber remembered that Crabtree "piled a group of young men in his car and drove them to Syracuse. It was illegal; no one was supposed to travel outside Oswego, but Crabtree wanted his students to see American industry at work. He took them into industrial plants and showed them such mind-boggling mechanical equipment that several decided that very day they would become engineers."[192]

Paul Bokros was one of those young men. Born in Belgrade, Yugoslavia, Paul's family was forced to leave Belgrade in the early 1940s. Paul and his

Shelter students gather on the steps of Oswego High School. Among those pictured are (*back row, left to right*) Eddie Levitch, Kostia Zabotin, Bruno Kaiser, Paul Bokros, Ralph Kuznitzki, Zachy Romano, Joseph Hirt, Jenny Bear, Gordana Milinovitch and Anita Baruch, with Alfons Finci standing behind; (*third row, left to right*): Ernst Spitzer and Nelly Bokros; (*second row, left to right*): Koki Levy, Leon Levitch, Alice Mandler, Rosa Moschev, Thea Weiss and Paul Arnstein; (*front row, left to right*): Ivo Lederer, Steffi Steinberg, Lea Hanf, Edith Weiss, Grete Spitzer and Ivo Svecenski. *Paradox*, 1945. *Oswego High School, Elaine Gagas Cost photograph.*

family then sought refuge throughout Europe, including in modern-day Croatia and Italy. The Bokros family members were among the 982 refugees brought to Fort Ontario. After graduating from Oswego High School in 1946, Paul and his family moved to Philadelphia.

In 1950, Paul enlisted in the United States Air Force. Following his service and honorable discharge as a sergeant, Paul took advantage of the GI Bill, graduating from La Salle University in Philadelphia with a bachelor of science degree in electronic physics.

In all, Paul spent over forty years working in the United States defense industry. Some of his projects included the design of digital communications for military aircraft, the Minutemen Missile Launch Control Center program and various NASA space programs. In the late 1970s, he joined General Dynamics in the electronics division in San Diego, where he rose to be the director of the F-16 Aircraft AIS Engineering program and division vice-president of operation. Paul was respected and admired throughout the industry for his exacting approach, a perfectionist's attention to detail and unflinching commitment to the highest of standards.[193]

Edward Levitch was drafted into the army, serving with the corps of engineers. After his service, he spent two years in Israel living in a kibbutz. Upon his return to the United States, Levitch established Levitch Associates, Architects and Contractors, fulfilling a calling to build that was perhaps first nurtured in Thomas Crabtree's industrial arts class.[194]

In an article for the *Ontario Chronicle* on April 26, 1945, Thomas Crabtree wrote, "It is hoped that through the efforts of the school the residents will find a new hope in the future and that skills learned or inspired will start them on the road to a better and happier life."[195] For Paul Bokros, Edward Levitch and others who came under Thomas Crabtree's influence, the Oswego High School experience did help lead them to a better and happier life.

OF ALL THE STUDENTS from the shelter who interacted with Ralph Faust at Oswego High School and after the shelter closed, Steffi Steinberg continued her friendship with Faust throughout his life.

Steinberg had fled Germany with her mother and father in the late 1930s. Her father left first, establishing a new business in Italy. Steffi and her mother followed. But soon after their arrival, Mussolini came out with new laws against the Jews. As the war enveloped Europe in 1940, her father had to give up the new business he had established, and the family was once again on the run. In June 1940, Steffi's father was seized, sent to an internment camp and died there later that year. Steffi and her mother stayed in Italy, evading the Nazis, until they were selected to board the transport ship *Henry Gibbins* and traveled with the 982 refugees bound for Fort Ontario.

Steinberg's time in Oswego and at the high school, she said, was "preparation for life."[196] Instrumental in shaping that experience, she said, was Ralph Faust and his work to support the refugee students in obtaining a high school diploma.

> [We] *went through the subjects in a very quick way and then in June 1945, Mr. Faust made it possible for us to take the Regents examination by having language exams come from Albany that we could take in order to give us the sufficient number of points. Of course, we all had very good previous education which helped us a great deal....So we took these... exams plus all the other subjects that we had taken in school and we passed the Regents...then graduated...and participated in the graduation ceremony....Throughout the whole thing Mr. Faust was just...a wonderful man who really put himself out without any personal gain to himself in any kind of way. He really is unique.*[197]

Steffi Steinberg and her mother moved to New York City after the shelter closed and Steffi had taken an advanced business course of studies at the Rochester Business Institute. She found work first as a waitress and secretary, and after a few years, she became an administrative assistant to an exporter. She married Sam Winters, a scrap metal dealer, and together, they raised three sons.

Loyal to the end to the wonderful man who had put himself out for the refugee students, Steffi Steinberg Winters was present for Ralph Faust's funeral services in August 1993.

Ralph Faust was an advocate for all the students he encountered during his long career in the Oswego City School District, where he served from 1939 until 1964. He is remembered whenever a production takes place at the theater at the Oswego High School that was named in his honor and in the Ralph and Dorothy Faust Rotary Scholarship that is awarded each year to a student who demonstrates potential to succeed in college. At the Safe Haven Holocaust Refugee Shelter Museum, he is remembered in the entry area, where a plaque, given in Mr. Faust's honor by the Fort Ontario Refugee Students of 1944–46, is prominently displayed. It reads, "For his guidance, encouragement, inspiration, and unstinting kindliness to us during our early days in our adopted homeland. Presented May 23, 1965." The museum

Edith Weiss, Lea Hanf and Steffi Steinberg at their high school graduation in 1945. *United States Holocaust Memorial Museum collection.*

also awards the Ralph Faust Humanitarian Award to honor individuals who have worked to improve the lives of refugees.[198]

"In Jewish lore we believe there are 36 souls that rule the earth," said Ruth Gruber. "Ralph Faust is one of those 36 souls. Ralph Faust helped the refugee students not only become citizens of America, but the kind of citizens that we all respect."[199]

Adult Education

The young people of the shelter were not the only ones interested in furthering their education. Many of their adult counterparts had been well-educated, practicing professionals before the war, but now, they found themselves in a new country where the next step in their lives was still very much uncertain.

When they were selected for transport to the United States, the 982 refugees were asked to sign a declaration form that at the end of the war, they would return to their home countries. Desperate to leave war-torn Europe and weary of the constant flight from Nazi forces, they signed the form. "During the period of selection, refugees frequently asked if they would be permitted to remain [in the United States]. In order to avoid misunderstanding, all persons coming to the Fort shelter were required to sign [a] statement, which was translated into German, French and Italian," wrote Edward Marks, the shelter's final director, in his book *Token Shipment.*

> *Section A I. of the statement read:*
> *"I shall be brought to a reception center in Fort Ontario in the State of New York where I shall remain as a guest of the United States until the end of the war. Then I must return to my homeland."*
>
> *In truth they expected, despite the statement they had signed, that they would have more freedom in this country than they had had abroad.*[200]

The refugees and the Oswego organizing committee did not wait for the federal government to decide their next step. The adults of the shelter wanted to learn English and engage in other educational programming as well. School district officials responded by enlisting a team of teachers who would provide English instruction at the shelter. By November 1944, more than five hundred shelter residents were learning to speak, read and write English in classes taught in the English Center at the fort. Twelve part-time teachers from the Oswego public schools conducted the classes.[201]

Muriel Perry was one of the twelve who was quick to respond. She recalled that she gave up her bowling night to serve. "We taught in the public schools in Oswego and were called in by the Superintendent to see if we'd like to take the job.…I gave up my bowling to do it and I never got back into it.…I don't regret it, for it was an experience well worthwhile."

After teaching all day in the junior high at Kingsford Park School, Perry ran home for supper and then traveled to the shelter, where English class for the adults began at 6:00 p.m. She normally stayed until 9:00 p.m.[202] Her classroom was an army room formerly used as a barracks, allowing enough room for just a picnic table with attached benches. Openings at the top of the side walls allowed for ventilation.[203]

"The first night I had 27 Yugoslavs and 18 Viennese, and I spoke not one word of their languages. It was very difficult at first…but about two in each group could speak a little English." Perry said early on there was a lot of pointing, and then she found that singing helped. "They knew some of our popular songs and 'The Star-Spangled Banner.'…And every song I taught them they enjoyed because the words, the pronunciation, came better."[204]

Perry's friend and colleague Frances Marion Brown taught English in the classroom adjoining Perry's. Brown recalled that Dr. Charles Riley, superintendent of the Oswego Schools, recruited teachers from the district who were already teaching English or speech and asked them to consider taking on instruction for the adults of the shelter. Dr. Riley felt that since the shelter children were in school and learning to speak English, their parents should learn English as well. Brown volunteered and remembered it was "a marvelous experience." She taught two classes at the shelter, one during the day and one at night. She recalled all the students in her classes were eager to learn. "We taught by talking and doing," said Brown. "We walk to the window. We walk to the door." Her students caught on quickly. "If you want to learn," said Brown, "you will."[205]

One evening around Christmas, Brown heard Perry trying to teach the song "Angels We Have Heard on High," but she was pairing it with the melody from a different song, "Mother Dear, O Pray for Me." Perry admitted she was not especially musical, but Frances Brown, when she heard Perry sing the wrong lyrics for the tune, came barreling into Perry's classroom, saying, "Goodness, sakes, what are you teaching?" "An unholy glee burst forth from the entire class because student Hugo Wantoch understood English and immediately translated [Brown's] remarks to all. It was the first truly jolly burst of laughter; their generally composed, worried looks disappeared, and it united class and teacher marvelously!"[206]

A more moving musical expression in Perry's class also occurred before the Christmas holiday. "I asked them to stand and sing 'The Star-Spangled Banner' and they did, and they were absolutely thrilled that they could do it....Then I turned to them, and I said, 'Sing your own national anthem.'" Amazed and somewhat hesitant, they asked Perry if this was truly possible. She assured them that it was indeed possible. "I said, 'You stand right there and do it.' And so, they did, and when they finished, they were all crying, and it was one of those moments where happiness was mingled with tears....I just stood. I didn't do anything else, and they were so proud of me because I stood for their national anthem, and I didn't know one word of it. And it was one of those things that I'll never forget."[207]

Both Perry and Brown entertained their adult students at their homes, forming personal friendships they both recalled fondly years later.[208] Brown remembered entertaining her students at her home and said that one man who had been in a concentration camp ultimately confided in her about his experience there. "He broke down when he told me what they did to him there," she said. And sadly, he died while at the shelter, succumbing to the injuries he had suffered in the concentration camp.[209]

Perry's eyes were opened to the security and bounty of America as well by the refugees. "They wanted to see people's homes," recalled Perry. "They wanted to get into people's homes to see what they were like inside." Perry invited some of her students for supper at her home. Her father had a new garden, and his prize strawberries were featured for dessert. She recalled they were thrilled with the first helping but more amazed that they could have seconds. Not only did Perry and her mother and father open their home for a tour for the students, but their neighbors Helen Orton and Helen Jermyn did as well. These people had not been in their own homes for a very long time, and, said Perry, they were curious whether European homes were different from American homes.

Perry kept in touch with many of these adult students after they left the shelter. She was especially fond of Hugo Wantoch, who she said was, "a dear friend, right from the beginning. He was…in his late seventies or going on eighty [and he] helped me to no end. He spoke English…quite well."

Hugo Wantoch appreciated the friendship with Perry and wrote a note to her about English class. "You wished to know why I attend the English classes. Well, there are several reasons. One of them is that I found a teacher, a magician who understands splendidly how to make us enjoy our English lessons, so that I, for instance, who detests nothing more than to sit quietly on the floor when to study when I was a little schoolboy, couldn't find at present a dearer hobby than to attend her class."[210]

Perry reflected years later that these experiences with the refugees emphasized for her what it truly means to be an American. "The daily pleasures like food, freedom of speech, religion…we as Americans take for granted were rare experiences for [these] Viennese and Yugoslavians."[211]

Jessie Wood Fleischman taught English at Oswego High School but volunteered for the evening English classes as well. She urged her students to write her letters to practice their English writing skills.

Alfredo Henle's letter from November 5, 1944, reflected his experience living at the shelter:

Dear Miss Wood,

In first time I will express my gratitude to the American government for have me allowed come in this beautiful country, during the World War, after so many unpleasantnesses in the camps of concentration in Italy…I am very happy that I can live now in peace.

Like Perry and Brown, Fleischman was happy to contribute, and though the teachers were eventually paid, her real remuneration was in the triumphs of her students as they began to master the English language.

By the late fall of 1944, the adult education opportunities for shelter residents were expanded with the addition of shop courses. Frank McPherson, a civilian employee at the shelter, would organize classes in machine shop practices, auto mechanics and carpentry. Leonard Jarvis was named the instructor for auto mechanics. A professional hygiene and beauty culture course was added under the direction of local beautician Mary Campo, and a class in sewing was started as well.[212]

Campo, a professional beautician, operated the Marmellow Beauty Shop on East Seneca Street. She taught interested refugee women the art of hair styling, manicures and facials. One of her star pupils was Edith Semjen,

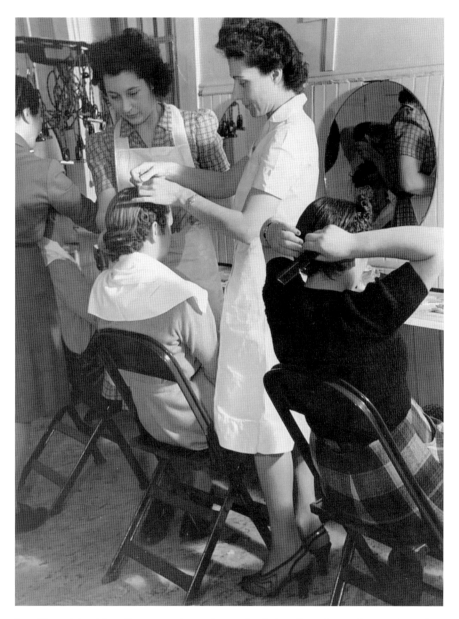

Local beautician Mary Campo teaches a class at the shelter. Forty-five students registered for the 240-hour course, and Ms. Campo said all were doing very well. *Gretchen VanTassel photograph, May 1945, Special Collections, Penfield Library, State University of New York at Oswego.*

Members of the shelter sewing class learn to use patterns under the guidance of Helen O'Brien. *Special Collections, Penfield Library, State University of New York at Oswego.*

Geri Desens Rossiter's great friend, who went on to own and operate one of Manhattan's most successful salons.

Helen O'Brien taught sewing for the shelter residents, conducting four classes daily with about eighteen students in each class.

Thomas Crabtree also extended his teaching services to the adults of the shelter. He wrote a story for the shelter newspaper, the *Ontario Chronicle*, encouraging more shelter residents to sign up for classes, because it was clear with the situation in Europe that many would be unable to return to their former occupations and professions. These classes, Crabtree noted, would provide new occupations and new talents. He arranged an exhibit of works by shelter residents already in the classes to encourage those who had not yet signed up to consider taking a class. "In our modern age," wrote Crabtree, "we are apt to view things through the eyes of mass production, and these messages from the old world could act as a reminder that there still is a joy in individual creation."[213]

Oswego photographer Frank Barbeau joined the cadre of local teachers at the shelter, expanding the adult class offerings with a class in photograph coloring, contributing the necessary supplies and many pictures to use for practice work. The instructor noted that "photo coloring, as any other art, affords an emotional release that could be beneficial in healing the wounds inflicted by the unhappy experiences of the past."

As an example, Barbeau told the story of one student whose husband had suffered terribly in the Buchenwald Concentration Camp. His experience left her without confidence, bitter and despairing. Prior to the war, this student had produced photography that won prizes in Europe. She was finally convinced to join the photograph coloring group. With help and encouragement, she regained her confidence, said the instructor, noting "the pride that glowed in her face as she showed me a country scene she had colored of her native Austria." It was, he said "ample compensation for the time and patience required in teaching her."[214]

Not only was Barbeau an excellent photographer, but he was a magician as well. The *Ontario Chronicle* of May 24, 1945, noted that Barbeau entertained the refugees with a variety of magic tricks at a party in honor of shelter director Joseph Smart. His performance was so well received that he was invited back to offer a repeat performance for shelter residents.[215]

The adult educators not only impacted the lives of their students for the better, but their own lives were also enriched in the process. Many stayed in touch with their refugee students for years after the shelter closed.

Frances Marion Brown said that her students emulated the Americans they encountered and were always so appreciative. They even tried to pay her with what little money they did have, but Brown refused. Still, at the Christmas holiday, all her students contributed to a gift for her: a beautiful comb and brush set that she treasured for the gesture it represented. She was, she reflected later, glad for the opportunity to teach the refugees. They caused her, she said, to "become more American, and to thank God for being an American."[216]

MURIEL PERRY CONTINUED TO teach English in the Oswego public schools. A former student, Keith Barron, acknowledged her influence on his choice of teaching as a career in a letter to the *Oswego County Messenger* in 1981. "Miss Perry's unrelenting willingness to help, breadth of knowledge in teaching, and trust in my own abilities, are the reasons for my successful completion of student teaching and graduation with a degree from Oswego State."[217]

Frances Marion Brown retired in 1979 after teaching for forty-two years at Kingsford Park School and Oswego High School. She was a founding member of the Oswego Players, a founding member of Arts and Culture for Oswego County and was Oswego's woman of the year in 1967. The Frances Marion Brown Theatre in Oswego is named in her honor.

Jessie Wood Fleischman taught English for forty-six years, retiring in 1968. She was invited to Albany for many summers to review Regents English test papers and to contribute questions for the Regents English examinations. The Jessie and Philip Fleischman Memorial Scholarship continues, each year, to support an Oswego High School student who has the potential to continue as a student athlete at the college level.

Thomas Crabtree was associated with the Oswego schools for almost fifty years. He retired as vocational education director for the school district. At age seventy-one, he established a school for practical nursing in Oswego. He was a navy veteran of World War I.

Frank Barbeau's Photography Studio was a fixture in Oswego's business community for many decades.

HIGHER EDUCATION

One of the most notable events at the Fort Ontario Emergency Refugee Shelter occurred in September 1944, just weeks after the 982 refugees arrived in Oswego. First Lady Eleanor Roosevelt made a visit to see for herself how the refugees were faring. She was accompanied by Mrs. Henry Morgenthau Jr., the wife of the secretary of the treasury. Mrs. Roosevelt and Mrs. Morgenthau visited both the shelter and the Oswego State Teachers College while in town.

Speaking at the shelter, Mrs. Roosevelt remarked that in greeting hundreds of the refugees, she had not received a single complaint, which she termed "unusual" and said that it spoke well for the success of the shelter. She acknowledged that the refugees at the fort were just "a drop in the bucket of suffering" and expressed hope that their presence in Oswego would build goodwill between Americans and people of other nations. "The Oswego committee has a real opportunity," she added, "and a real obligation to let the rest of the people of the United States know about our guests. We all have an obligation to create good will throughout the nation. Without good will throughout the world," she concluded, "there is no chance of lasting peace."[218]

After lunch and entertainment at the shelter, Mrs. Roosevelt and Mrs. Morgenthau visited the Oswego State Teachers College, where college president Ralph Swetman noted in his greeting how fitting it was in Mrs. Roosevelt's presence as first lady and one of the country's great leaders that she be welcomed by the president of the student body, "the first lady of our college—Miss Betty Burden."

Left: Dr. Ralph Swetman, Oswego Teachers College president, escorts First Lady Eleanor Roosevelt. *Ontarion*, 1945. *Special Collections, Penfield Library, State University of New York at Oswego.*

Opposite: Student body president Betty Burden and student Carol McLaughlin greet First Lady Eleanor Roosevelt as she enters Sheldon Hall at the Oswego Teachers College. *Ontarion*, 1945. *Special Collections, Penfield Library, State University of New York at Oswego.*

Burden noted that Eleanor Roosevelt "is one of the greatest women in the world and has set an outstanding record in world affairs. The women of our college," continued Burden, "since the outbreak of war, have also been required to…set a high standard in school affairs."

Although men normally constituted a majority of the college's enrollment, they were then serving in the armed forces, and, said Burden, "the women have been forced to carry on…filling their responsibilities and duties to the best of our ability."[219]

During her tour of the shelter, Mrs. Roosevelt encountered twenty-two-year-old refugee David Levy, who was convalescing in the fort hospital. When she asked what he needed, his response was immediate. He wanted to be able to attend college.[220] In an interview years later, Levy said that he "expressed to her his dream of attending college and making something important happen in his life." His eyes teared up as he recalled meeting the first lady, describing her as "warm and kind and very concerned for young people." She promised to help the refugees attend college and made good on that promise.[221]

Though elementary, junior high and high school students were already in local classrooms, college-aged refugees had missed the start of the fall semester at the college. With a boost from Mrs. Roosevelt, however, arrangements were

made to admit those wishing to attend the college for the spring 1945 semester. The college would prove pivotal in the lives of those students.

Oswego was also the place Levy first met his wife, Zdenka Ruchwager. Zdenka was a young woman married to a fellow refugee and doctor. Levy, who was single at the time, was a patient in the hospital. In time, David and Zdenka were reunited after Levy's divorce and after the death of Zdenka's first husband. David recounted that a neighbor of his mother from New York knew Zdenka and said that she was widowed. She told David's mother she had the perfect person for him and arranged a meeting between the two in Washington, D.C., where Zdenka was then living. "I fell in love the first time I saw her," said David.[222]

Fifty-seven years after the shelter closed, David and Zdenka returned to the college campus for an event to kick off the inaugural Oswego Reading Initiative, titled "An Evening with David Levy: Memories of Safe Haven, Oswego and Oswego State." Former Oswego State classmate Carol Rosenberg introduced Levy as both "a serious student and ping-pong champion." The Levys, said Rosenberg, were "two of the 982 refugees that exemplify the treasures that were spared" from the war and the Holocaust. Rosenberg recalled David Levy as "a firecracker, like a burst of energy. You could always tell when David was around."

Shelter students were admitted to the Oswego Teachers College for the 1945 spring semester. Pictured on the steps of Sheldon Hall (*left to right*) are Sami Romano, Tina Korner, Jetta Hendel, David Levy, Mira Lederer, Walter Mauer and Alexander Margulies. *Special Collections, State University of New York at Oswego.*

Levy told the audience at the event that he never forgot the wonderful, dedicated, patient and kind teachers he encountered at the college, many of whom went above and beyond to help the refugee students.[223] He singled out Dr. Seward Salisbury from the college for initiating meetings between the college refugee students and the American students through socials. Levy recalled that because so many of the male college students were away in service, the "sorority ladies" asked the male refugee students to be their dates for social events. He laughed about the cost for flowers and a taxi service, but he said it was a very nice experience just the same.

Zdenka was experiencing a different kind of social life during that time. She and her husband, who was older, worked at the fort hospital, and when there was an opportunity for down time, they took advantage of events taking place at the shelter theater or socialized with the other doctors and their wives who lived at the shelter.

Zdenka recalled Oswego as a magical scene in the winter, with snow covering everything; she especially remembered the Christmas lights on the houses and in the downtown area, something they never saw in Europe during the war. Seeing the turn of the seasons and the celebrations of Palm Sunday and Easter gave a sense of wonder and normalcy that had been missing from her life for so long. She was also amazed at the bounty available in the local A&P Grocery Store, and seeing their fully stocked grocery shelves, she said, was "incredible."

David and Zdenka both experienced fear and flight while in war-torn Europe. David's father was a lawyer who opposed the Nazis, but he died before he could be seized. That made David fair game, but his mother managed to obtain false papers for him, allowing him to escape. He eventually made his way to Rome and was then selected to join the

982 Holocaust refugees who were transported to the United States and eventually to the Fort Ontario Emergency Refugee Shelter. David came alone. His family all perished in Europe.[224]

Zdenka's family was well-to-do and comfortable in Zagreb, Yugoslavia, before the Nazis marched in. Zdenka, along with her mother, father and brother, experienced abuse, humiliation and separation in concentration camps before making their way to the Ferramonti Camp in Italy. The camp was finally liberated by British forces. "It was absolutely wonderful," Zdenka said. "I can picture them today. All these young soldiers in uniforms. Coming out with knapsacks full of food and distributing Spam and chocolates and other things. We were just elated." At Ferramonti, Zdenka met her first husband, physician Abraham Ruchwager, and they, too, were among the 982 refugees selected for transport to the United States.[225]

Though their lives took different paths at the shelter and in the years after, David and Zdenka ultimately found each other again and agreed that the Oswego experience was transformative.

David obtained a bachelor's degree from Case Western Reserve University after moving to Cleveland. He received help completing his degree from the Jewish community there, eventually relocating to San Francisco.

Zdenka continued to work as a nurse and joined David in San Francisco after they were married.[226]

DR. SEWARD SALISBURY, WHO provided David Levy and the other refugee students at the college with the opportunity to interact with their American counterparts, was among a group of college faculty who went beyond their classroom duties to serve the refugee students. Along with colleagues Marion Mahar, Charles Wells and Aulus Saunders, he embraced the shelter population and worked hard to provide opportunities for advancement. Salisbury recalled, "We tried to bring them into the college community socially....In the spring we had a senior party and dance at our house.... We had one of those big old houses and we could open some of the sliding doors, so we had a great deal of room. These students came...and everyone interacted, danced....I'd say the social aspects [of college] were probably more important than the educational aspects...and it was educational to us; we learned something from it."[227]

Salisbury joined his colleagues Dr. Charles Wells and Professor Marion Mahar to serve the entire adult refugee population by creating a series of lectures on the American way of life. The lectures were meant to acquaint the refugees with the culture and customs of the United States. Their "Culture of America" forums were held at the shelter with a guest lecturer each week on a particular topic relating to American life. Dr. Wells directed the forums, and a number of Oswegonians took part as lecturers. Salisbury conducted the history of the United States lecture; Marion Mahar discussed political parties and the election, as well as minorities in America; and Saunders lectured on art in America. The college trio launched the weekly lectures in late October 1944, and they continued until March 1945.[228]

Among the college faculty members, there was likely none more familiar with the conditions in Europe under Nazi occupation than Marion Mahar. She had studied at the University of Berlin in 1937 and 1938 and witnessed the rise of Adolf Hitler and the Nazi Party. In a series of lectures upon her return from Germany, Mahar warned of potential perils to come.

At a meeting of the Oswego Women's City Club in November 1938, Mahar spoke of Germany as she saw it during her stay there and her witnessing of the mass rallies that marked the rise of national socialism. "It is just like a beehive. All the people I saw there were working with one idea, to make Germany a great power again....However, there exists an undercurrent of excitement, just like being on top of a volcano, and never quite knowing when it will erupt." She described crowds as large as two hundred thousand gathering for demonstrations with a military-like character. "It is this desire for a super-race that prompts them to deny citizenship to all non-Aryan peoples, who have no place in their scheme of world power."[229]

Marion Mahar joined the social studies faculty at the college in 1931, teaching courses in social studies, public speaking and German and English literature. She was respected, admired and loved by the students who studied under her. "With hair flying and fired with enthusiasm, Marion Mahar holding forth in a classroom was a wonder to behold. A thrilling teacher," recalled an Oswego alumna.[230]

During the war years, Mahar accepted heavier teaching loads to compensate for the loss of so many of the male faculty members to the armed services. In addition to assisting Wells and Salisbury with the American culture lecture series, she served on the Oswego Citizens Advisory Committee, focusing on the education of the children at the shelter and working with newspaper publisher Edwin Waterbury on the rumor subcommittee.[231] Marion Mahar had a special reason to be "fired with enthusiasm" to assist the refugees. She knew full well what they had escaped.

Aulus Saunders was the head of the Art Department at the college. When the refugees arrived, Saunders and his daughter Susan went to the fort to greet them. Susan took along a doll she owned. Saunders recalled later, "I think she took it because she possibly had in mind…giving it to one of the children." Susan did just that, handing the doll over to a little girl from Austria.[232] "Later in the afternoon, when press photographers learned of the incident, they sought out the two girls to make pictures of Susan presenting the doll to the refugee girl. When the doll was taken and handed back to Susan to go through the act again the refugee cried loudly. However, the newsmen quickly smoothed things over when they made their 'shots' and returned the doll to the sobbing child from far away Austria."[233]

The Saunders family would have more interactions with the refugees, particularly with the Kuttner family. Siegfried Kuttner was also an artist and a stage designer. Despite his prominence as a professor of stage design in Germany, he was forced to flee the Nazi advance. Aulus Saunders met Siegfried Kuttner when he went to the fort to discuss the need for art supplies for the refugees. Kuttner was the leader in this area.

Saunders recalled their first meeting. Kuttner was not available when Saunders arrived, but he did meet Peter Kuttner, Siegfried's son, and got into a game of chess with the young man. "This was our introduction," said Saunders, "and a very pleasant one. We later went out on sketching trips around the town and in the country together."

The Kuttners were guests at the Saunders home on many occasions, along with others from the fort.[234]

While Aulus and Siegfried worked together to obtain art supplies and set up studios for the twenty-four refugee artists, their sons Alan and Peter struck up a friendship. "Peter and I used to play in the dungeons at the Fort, back when you could wander around any place you wanted to," Alan remembered.

Aulus Saunders felt that the artists who had fled persecution in Europe might interest Americans in their story with a significant message for the world through their art. He arranged for exhibits of their artwork to be featured at the shelter and at the college. In June 1945, the director of the Syracuse Art Museum, now the Everson Museum of Art, visited the shelter to choose entries for the arts and crafts exhibition planned for that museum. The exhibit was eventually taken to New York City for display as well.[235]

The leadership of college president Ralph Swetman, along with the contributions of faculty members like Seward Salisbury, Charles Wells, Marion Mahar and Aulus Saunders, allowed the refugee students at the college to thrive. Though none desired to become teachers, they took foundational courses that moved them to the next steps in their educational pursuits.

Brothers Aca and Rajko Margulis had studied medicine at the University of Belgrade in Yugoslavia before the war forced them from their homeland. Both gained admission to Harvard Medical School based on their high marks in Oswego. Shelter rules and family concerns initially prevented them from attending Harvard, but they were eventually able to obtain Harvard Medical School degrees.

The Margulis brothers credited Dr. Swetman and their Oswego education for putting them on solid academic footing. In a letter to Swetman, they wrote, "Leaving this country we desire to express to you once more our deep gratitude for all the kindness you have showed us. We shall never forget the friendly atmosphere we enjoyed while attending the Oswego State Teachers College. We know that we have sincere friends in Oswego who tried their best, as you did, to help us. It was really a pleasure to study in a school led by you."[236]

The college held a special assembly at the time of the Victory in Europe celebration, and Swetman recounted a talk given by Alex (Aca) Margulis to those assembled. Margulis talked about his background and about the last six or seven years he had spent in war-torn Europe. "He spoke with such force and fire, and he is a fine speaker," said Swetman. "During the time he was speaking, and there were 400 students in the assembly, you could hear a pin drop."[237]

Ralph (Rajko) Margulis graduated first in his class from Harvard Medical School, despite having to learn the English language from a dictionary. Following medical school, he completed his residency in obstetrics and gynecology at Henry Ford Hospital in Detroit. During more than forty years practicing medicine, he delivered four generations of babies, primarily in Oakland County. Ralph was head of the OB/GYN Department at William Beaumont Hospital in Royal Oak, Michigan, for over eighteen years and served as vice–chief of staff at Beaumont for many years. Ralph founded one of the first HMOs in Michigan, as well as the largest physicians' organization in the state. A pioneer in his field, Ralph developed new cancer treatments for women and was dedicated to women's health issues.[238]

Alex (Aca) Margulis "was a global visionary leader of radiology, beloved by physicians at UCSF and throughout the world," according to a tribute posted by Dr. William Dillon on the University of California at San Francisco radiology blog upon Alex Margulis's passing. He was, wrote Dr. Dillon, "beloved by physicians at UCSF and throughout the world. Alex touched the lives and careers of innumerable radiologists and scientists, and he enriched us all with his humor, leadership, and sagacious support of imaging science. He was the heart of UCSF Radiology for the 26 years of his chairmanship that spanned 1963 to 1989. He led the extraordinary evolution of imaging that began with the early days of CT, MRI, US, PET-CT, interventional radiology, molecular imaging, and other modalities. His impact on the health of individuals everywhere and the careers of myriad radiologists in the United States and abroad cannot be overstated."[239]

Oswego, Alex said, "was one of my most wonderful experiences. We young people were happy. It was an island of plenty."[240]

Seward Salisbury, Marion Mahar and Aulus Saunders continued to serve and inspire several generations of college students. Awards established in their honor continue to support students at SUNY Oswego today. Seward Salisbury retired to North Carolina after a long and distinguished teaching career. Dr. Ralph Swetman retired as president of the college in 1947 and moved with his wife to Florida. Swetman Hall, completed in 1963, was named in his honor. The building has since been merged into the new Campus Center. Mahar Hall, named in honor of Marion Mahar, opened in 1966 and continues as an academic building on the campus today. Aulus Saunders continued as chairman of the Art Department until 1970. In 1957, he hired famed artist Roy Lichtenstein, who taught in the art department until 1960. The Saunders family remained actively involved in the Oswego community and maintained their friendship with the Kuttner family after they relocated, and Siegfreid obtained a teaching position at the University of Texas. Saunders recalled that Kuttner sent him a nice letter of appreciation and enclosed a photograph of himself wearing a ten-gallon hat. Saunders said, "I thought, 'Well now, there is really a transformation from the middle of Europe to Texas with the ten-gallon hat!'"[241]

The International Scout Troops

Harold Clark, the Fitzgibbons boiler plant worker who had looked out on the survivors of Hitler's horrors the day the refugees arrived and asked himself what he might possibly do to help, was the leader of Boy Scout Troop 19 in Minetto, a village just a short drive from the city of Oswego.

In late September 1944, Kenneth Lawrence, a civilian employee at the shelter and a local Cub Scout master, had gathered a small group of boys to collect wastepaper for the war effort. His small team organized into a Scout group, and permission was requested to establish a troop at the fort. Although the national Boy Scout regulations required Scouts to be United States citizens, citizenship requirements were waived for this special case. Lawrence began to organize the troop.[242]

Ferdinand Kaska, the youth director of the shelter, served as the translator, with Kenneth Lawrence serving as Scoutmaster for what became Cub Pack No. 3, and Harold Clark joined the effort as Scoutmaster for what became Boy Scout Troop 28, the world's first international Boy Scout troop.

Kaska recalled that Clark "came even in the worst possible of Oswego weather to work with our boys and the boys in turn are as fond of him as of a brother."[243] Harold Clark worked all day welding tanks and aircraft carrier parts at the Fitzgibbons plant but saw the kids gathered at the shelter fence on his lunch breaks. "I guess I had compassion for them," Clark recalled. "I knew they didn't have very much, and I thought that here was an opportunity....I thought that it'd be good for some of the boys of our [Minetto] troop [to] be leaders there and have the experience." Clark asked for volunteers from

Cub Scout Troop 3 at the Fort Ontario Emergency Refugee Shelter. *Front row, left to right*: Jakov Kampos, Wilhelm Wittenberg, Milan Polijokan, Silvestro Wachsmann and Miko Finzi. *Second row, left to right*: Walter Grunberg, Nikola Marinkovic, Miroslav Lang, Kenneth Lawrence, Ferdinand Kaska, Heinz Grun, Josef Hazan and Erik Levy. *Third row, left to right*: Branko Hochwald, Michael Hirt, Julius Krauthamer, Jakov Levi (possibly), Walter Cohen, Pietri Albrecht and two unidentified boys. *United States Holocaust Memorial Museum.*

Troop 19, and he had so many that, he said, "right away I had to do some picking and selecting."

Clark and three or four of his Scouts would drive to the fort weekly. The excitement of the boys in the shelter who joined Clark's troop was palpable. Clark remembers that "they didn't want us to leave; they'd climb all over [my] car on the fender and everything." What impressed him more than anything was the refugee boys' discipline and work ethic. In the early weeks of the troop, while still in need of an interpreter, they were able to play games and engage in the typical Scouting activities. "We'd play games where they had to get down on the floors on their hands and knees sometimes, and of course the floors hadn't been dusted in years, an old Army barracks, and before we'd do anything else outside of the games, they'd raise their hands, and through the interpreter, ask permission to first wash their hands." Their American counterparts, said Clark, just rubbed their dirty hands on their pants.

The new Scouts shared stories of their experiences in Europe sleeping on the floor, on straw, on sidewalks in the streets where they came from, and they just could not get over, when they did get to Fort Ontario, that there were mattresses for them to sleep on. "These were things we all took for granted," said Clark.

He also recalled that the shelter boys were more eager and more aggressive about engaging in every activity. "Our boys [took] things as a 'so-what' attitude….These fellows were denied those things…but now, coming [to the United States] this was new and how they ate that Scouting program up!"

The international troop provided many memorable experiences for Clark and the members of his Minetto troop. The shelter boys took a train from Oswego the six or seven miles to Minetto and then hiked up in the woods along a railroad track to cook out with the Minetto Scouts. Clark laughed recalling one breakfast that was cooked by the two troops. "Course there's two kinds of Jewish people, Reformed and Orthodox, which I know, and I had to laugh at one of these [shelter Scouts]. I stood over him, he had this big frying pan with slab bacon. I cleared my throat, and I called him by name, Eric, and I says, 'What's…?' He says, 'I know what you're gonna' say.' 'Yeah, how come the bacon,' asked Clark, to which the Scout replied, 'We like it!'" And that, concluded Clark, was all that mattered.

Clark said his only desire was to give the boys from the shelter a good time and teach them about America through Scouting. His Minetto Scouts and the shelter Scouts shared cooking and hiking and earned badges together. In the end, said Clark of the Minetto Scouts, "Those boys with me got as much out of it, maybe more, than I did."[244]

Eric Levy, the shelter Scout who liked bacon, and Mirko (Mike) Nussbaum served as patrol leaders for the shelter troop. They reported on a fourteen-mile hike taken in August 1945. Their trek began at the shelter, continued up the east side of the Oswego River, over the bridge at Minetto and then back down the west side of the river to the fort. A woman driving by them on the east side of the river stopped to offer the hikers a ride. The pair explained that this was a hike required for their Scout program, thanked her for the offer and continued on their way. It took them the better part of a day, but the boys were determined to complete the assignment for the man all the boys came to fondly call "Clarkie."[245]

Walter Greenberg was part of Clark's troop and recalled his Scoutmaster as a very nice man who spent a lot of time with the boys of the shelter troop. He said that he didn't realize until years later how the Scouting experience had influenced him as a person. "First of all, I was part of a Boy Scout Troop; I was also a leader in the Cub Scouts. I was very active. I was very proud of my uniform coming from a kind of place where uniforms meant terror. To have my uniform which meant goodness, be prepared, help others, don't cheat, and all the values [of] the Boy Scouts, [as well as] the love of nature, which I liked."

Erik Levy, patrol leader, Troop 23, January 1946. *Harold Clark Collection, Special Collections, Penfield Library, State University of New York at Oswego.*

Greenberg described Clark:

> *In a way,* [he was] *a father to us, the way our parents or fathers couldn't perform. Not that they didn't perform well, but on a different level, because he had lived his normal life in a free society, and he was fun to be with. It was a good, happy time. I remember we had to go on a hike and a friend of mine had to go. We were told…if anybody wants to pick you up, you are not allowed to hitch-hike. We were Boy Scouts and in order to get a badge, you have to walk, and this car stopped, and he asked us to come in. We were very indignant, and we said, "No, we can't, we have to do the right thing," and I think that stayed with me, to do the right thing.*[246]

Harold Clark recalled a variety show that the Minetto troop sponsored in October 1945, complete with a color guard ceremony. Eric Levy brought in the Yugoslavia flag, and one of the Minetto Scouts carried the American flag.

Boy Scout Troop 28 at the Fort Ontario Emergency Refugee Shelter. *Front row, left to right*: S. Schwarzenberg, W. Greenberg, C. Boni and T. Danon. *Second row, left to right*: S. Boni, M. Kahmi, E. Hibberd, F. Felice, F. Kaska, H. Clark, J. Flannigan and M. Nussbaum. *Third row, left to right*: D. Hajon, F. Flatau, J. Bronner, Y. Urdian, E. Levy and R. Flatau. *Safe Haven Holocaust Refugee Shelter Museum.*

"Then we all had flags, through the Scout council, of the United Nations. It was a very, very impressive opening ceremony," recalled Clark. "I never saw one since to compare with it."[247]

The excitement of Scouting ultimately spilled over to the girls of the shelter as well. With the coming of the first full summer at the shelter, it was clear the young people, once out of school, would need activities to keep them occupied. Shelter resident Fortunee Levitch organized a Girl Scout troop. At the same time, a group of young adults working with the Quakers came to the fort to assist for the summer.[248] They would prove to be excellent mentors for the shelter youth, and prominent among the mentors was a young woman from Vicksburg, Mississippi, named Esther Morrison. Tall, with brown eyes and a southern drawl, Esther Morrison arrived with a master's degree in social work and lots of experience working with young people. Ruth Gruber recalled that she instantly made the young girls of the shelter feel safe and happy. "She led children whose earliest memories were of flight and hunger and fear into the security of American life."[249]

Esther Danon was one of those children. Her family experienced Nazi sympathizers bursting into their synagogue in the Yugoslavian city of Split, wielding bayonets, beating people and burning sacred texts. Esther's father and brother joined the Partisans, while Esther, her mother and older sister hid on a farm with a sympathetic woman who had delivered their milk. Esther recalled living in a closet for six months when she was seven, forced to keep quiet to stay safe from Nazis and Nazi sympathizers. She said it wasn't hard for her to keep quiet. "When you live in those circumstances in the middle of the war, you grow up fast, I knew what was going on—not a word escaped my lips."

Eventually, the Germans began asking too many questions, and the family had to leave. The milk lady's husband offered to take them to a cousin's house on a nearby island, where they stayed for three more months. But when that grew too dangerous, they were put out. Their only option was to climb into the mountains. The climb was hard, without a path; the girls wore dresses, and their legs quickly grew bloody.

Partisan fighters took in refugees, and Esther, her mother and sister spent months with them. During the day, they would hide from the Germans who patrolled the skies; at night, they would move in lines, with resistance fighters in the front and back with rifles to protect them. Their food was flour mixed with water; sometimes there was nothing to eat. Once, it rained for a week straight—the family used their single blanket as a makeshift roof when they could.

The family finally made their way to an Italian refugee camp, where they got word that Esther's brother and father were in a nearby city and had been chosen to go to the United States.[250] Finally united, the Danon family was among the 982 refugees who traveled to the Fort Ontario Emergency Refugee Shelter. There, Esther would meet Esther Morrison, the young woman who would make her feel safe and happy at last.

Mona Lisa Gioconda, the young daughter of shelter artist Miriam Sommerburg, remembered Esther Morrison fondly as well and continued a friendship with her throughout her life. She was, said Mona, "one of the centers of interest at the camp," and "she was a tremendous person."

The youngest of Miriam's five children, Mona Lisa was so named because her mother thought she looked like DaVinci's *Mona Lisa* when she was born. Miriam was an acclaimed artist, married to Rudolph, a journalist, when the Nazis came to power. Rudolph was a blond, blue-eyed Aryan German. Miriam was a dark-haired Jewish woman. Rudolph became very critical of Hitler, so the family was eventually escorted to the French border and banished from Germany. In France, Miriam and Rudolph separated, and Miriam made her way south into Italy with her children. Four of the five children traveled with Miriam on the *Henry Gibbins* to Fort Ontario in Oswego. The oldest went with the British army.

At the fort, Mona Lisa came under Esther Morrison's spell, like many of the other young girls who spent time with her. "Oswego gave us respite," said Mona Lisa. And Esther Morrison certainly played a big part in providing that respite.[251]

Girl Scout Troop 40, Refugee Shelter, the newest of the seventeen Girl Scout troops in the Oswego area, was announced by district chairman Mrs. Francis T. Riley, with Miss Esther Morrison as the leader.[252]

Esther was not just a great mentor; she was resourceful as well. When she was told there was no money for uniforms for the girls, Esther brought the girls to her apartment and taught them to bake cookies, which they then sold in town. They earned enough money to purchase scarves and pins, which they wore proudly.[253]

Esther Danon Kaidanow recalled Esther Morrison's kindness years later, recounting the day when Esther announced there was still a bit of money left in the troop coffers after the purchase of scarves and pins. "One day she asked [the girls], 'Who has family in Europe?' She then produced a bunch of straws and announced that the one who picked the shortest straw would win a package that Esther would arrange to send to family abroad."

Nine-year-old Esther Danon won the drawing, and a silk blouse was purchased in town, packed and sent to her oldest sister, who was still in Yugoslavia with the Partisans. "Little Esther had learned that her 17-year-old sister had been wounded in the fighting and was destitute. The blouse became a symbol among the Partisans; whoever had a birthday wore the blouse from Fort Ontario, America."[254]

On January 10, 1946, representatives from the Girl Scout troops of the Oswego-Minetto district, along with their leaders made the fourth Girl Scout law, "A Girl Scout is a friend to all and a sister to every other Girl Scout," a reality as they welcomed the thirteen girls of the shelter troop and their leader into the Girl Scout circle.

Parents of the girls were present to hear their daughters take the Girl Scout promise and be brought into the sisterhood of more than one million girls throughout the United States. In speaking to the parents, Mrs. Hollis Greenman, deputy commissioner, said, "In whatever community of the United States they settle, when they leave Fort Ontario, they will find a Girl Scout troop and friends."[255]

In addition to the Girl Scout troop, Morrison organized ping-pong tournaments, other games, evening activities and sing-alongs. At other times, recalled Sylvain Boni, who was a member of the Boy Scout troop, she would just sit and talk with the kids. "We felt privileged to have someone who understood us and cared for us, seeing to it that we spent our time constructively. Long after we had left Oswego, we corresponded with Esther and enjoyed several visits from her."[256]

MAY 1945 SAW THE end of the war in Europe. It was news received with great joy and great trepidation at the Emergency Refugee Shelter. President Roosevelt had died, and President Truman was left with the question of what to do about the 982 "guests of the United States" at Fort Ontario, the majority of whom wanted to remain in the United States despite having signed the declaration form stating they would return to their home countries after the war.

On June 25 and 26, Congressman Samuel Dickstein convened a hearing at the fort to investigate the problems presented by refugees at the fort shelter. This was an opportunity for those wishing to remain in the United States to make their case to Dickstein's congressional committee. Testifying on the first day were fourteen members of Troop 28.

Walter Greenberg was one of the Scouts who appeared before the committee. It was, he remembered, a defining moment for the refugees, particularly the Boy Scouts. "We paraded in uniform with the American flag and the troop flag, and we recited the Boy Scout Oath," he said. "We were paraded in a positive way to show the congressmen how well we had acclimated ourselves to American life and American customs. I'm sure that this had a positive effect on the subcommittee."[257]

Chairman Dickstein questioned each boy in turn, asking their ages, where they had come from in Europe and whether they wished to remain in the United States. In addition, they were asked, if they were allowed to remain in the country, would they be willing to take up arms to defend the United States. Eric Levy, Mirko Nussbaum and Walter Greenberg each testified, giving a brief summary of their experiences in war-torn Europe and affirming their desire to stay in the United States.[258]

It would take another six months before the question of whether the 982 would be allowed to stay in the United States was resolved, but the boys of Troop 28 had convinced Congressman Dickstein and his committee that they should.

Once the shelter did close, Harold Clark's Boy Scouts continued to correspond with him. Several sought out troops in their new cities and asked Clark to send them news from his troop and his photograph so they could remember him. Clark wrote to them once they settled in their new homes.

The shelter boys heard that Clark was awarded Boy Scouting's highest honor, the Silver Beaver Award, for his leadership of Troop 28. They wrote letters of congratulations to him. "I am proud that of the few Scoutmasters, mine received the highest award in Scouting and I am honored that you were my Scoutmaster," wrote Moric Kamhi.[259]

Clark continued to make the members of the first international Boy Scout troop proud with his advocacy for bringing the lessons of Scouting to underserved populations. Each summer, Oswego was home to migrant workers and their families who relocated to the area temporarily to harvest local crops. In the summer of 1959, Clark worked with the sons of migrant workers to introduce them to Boy Scouting.

The boys were sons of the workers at the Lockwood, Patane, Chillson Labor Camps at North Hannibal, a short drive from the city of Oswego. Clark again enlisted members of his Minetto Troop 19 to assist. From July 13 to August 17, the migrant boys were instructed, and each completed the Tenderfoot requirements. "It is thought by the migrant committee that Troop 19 is the only troop in New York State which includes migrant Boy Scouts," reported the *Palladium-Times*. "The boys originally from Florida, will be issued transfer blanks at the end of August prior to their return south to enable them to continue Scouting there and then return again [to Oswego] the next summer. The ages range from 11 to 16 years and these boys are enthusiastically taking to the Scout program."[260]

After the members of his international troop left Oswego, Clark predicted success for each of them. "I know that they've become good citizens, wherever they are, and I'm only happy that I had a share in [the] formation of their citizenship."[261]

Clark was certainly right about the members of Troop 28.

Mirko (Mike) Nussbaum went on to earn a bachelor's degree in physics and mathematics from Rutgers University, a master's degree at the University of Chicago and a doctorate at Johns Hopkins University. He also worked as a physics instructor at Johns Hopkins University and as a research associate at Columbia University before becoming an assistant professor at the University of Pennsylvania. He joined the University of Cincinnati as an associate professor and then became a full professor in 1971. He was named a fellow of the American Physical Society in 1973 for his research accomplishments. One of Nussbaum's most important research achievements came while he was a graduate student, when he helped to discover a new subatomic particle known as the eta particle. This was the start of a long and productive career doing research in high energy particle physics, said Louis Witten, professor emeritus, who was the department head in physics when Nussbaum came to the University of Cincinnati. Nussbaum continued exploring particle physics for the next thirty years as part of the collaborative teams at the world's leading physics research facilities, such as the Fermi National Accelerator Laboratory near Chicago and the European Center for Nuclear Research in Geneva, Switzerland. Sadly, he perished in a private plane crash on April 8, 1997, at the age of sixty-six.[262]

Eric Levy Lee became a gastroenterologist and served as the director of medical education in the Kaiser Permanente Medical Group in Bellflower, California. He also served as an associate clinical professor at UCLA.

Walter Greenberg and his parents moved to New York City, where he became a documentary filmmaker and optical effects producer. As an administrator at Rockman Community College, he founded the college's food resource center, a job that returned him to Oswego in October 1984 for a conference on university housing. He found great satisfaction in resolving housing problems for others. "A kid who came hungry…without shoes…I had come full circle."[263]

Esther Danon moved with her family to Philadelphia when the shelter closed. She graduated from high school, married Howard Kaidanow, also a Holocaust survivor, and raised a family. As of this writing, she and her husband live in Maryland, and Esther continues to participate in presentations about her experiences during World War II.

Harold Clark continued to mentor generations of Scouts as Scoutmaster to more than four thousand Boy Scouts in Minetto and Oswego.[264] In addition to the Silver Beaver Award, Scouting's highest honor, he received the Scouter's key for training courses. He was named "Man of the Year" by the Oswego Jaycees for 1961–62. An amateur photographer, Clark presented slide programs to area nursing homes, churches and civic organizations. He was also the Minetto town historian.[265]

Esther Morrison had come to the fort after graduating from Mississippi State College for Women and earning a master's degree from the University of Louisville. She went on to earn a doctorate in ancient history and far eastern languages at Harvard University. In the late 1940s, she worked with the YWCA in China, where she offered special leadership training for women. She taught at the University of California at Berkeley until 1963, when she moved to Washington, D.C., and joined the faculty at Howard University. She retired from Howard in 1980. A visionary who was always ahead of her time, Esther Morrison founded the Capitol Hill Recycling Project with the help of the National Association of Black Veterans of Washington. She ran one of the most successful recycling centers in the D.C. metropolitan area.[266]

The Loudest Voices

The members of Troop 28 were effective voices for the argument to allow the 982 residents of the Emergency Refugee Shelter to remain in the United States, but they were joined in a chorus by many of the Oswegonians who had come to know the refugees during the months they lived at the fort.

Once the quarantine was lifted and the school-age students at the shelter entered local classrooms, more connections developed between shelter residents and the people of the city. In the waning months of 1944, adult residents of the shelter were invited as guests at events sponsored by local civic and religious organizations.

The St. Paul's Church Young Women's Club held a breakfast and invited a group of women from the shelter as their guests. Club members subsequently invited the women to join the organization during their stay in Oswego.[267]

The Faculty Wives Club at the teachers' college invited shelter director Joseph Smart and shelter resident Mrs. Siegfried Kuttner to their first meeting of the season. Mrs. Kuttner shared an exhibit of artwork done by twelve German and Italian artists at the shelter, some completed by the artists while in a concentration camp in Italy.[268]

Steven Koen of Yugoslavia, who had been a Rotarian there until forced to flee the Nazis, spoke at a meeting of the Oswego Rotary Club. He gave a moving speech, touching on the theme of Rotary, which was "international understanding, good will, and peace through a world fellowship of business and professional men united in the ideal of service." Koen was a charter member of the Rotary Club of Belgrade and had participated in Rotary conferences throughout Europe. "Mr. Koen…told how he found a fellow Rotarian from Spalato [Split], a famous lawyer, who risked his existence and property to help him by testifying before authorities that they were the persons they claimed to be, although he knew their names were false," said a report on Koen's speech in the *Palladium-Times*. "When his friend told him that he risked his existence and property to help me," Mr. Koen said, "he answered: 'I know it, but the lives of my friends are in question, and I must make all to save them. Also, Rotarian Koen would do the same for me, if necessary.'" So, concluded Koen to those assembled, "I lived to see that Rotary friendship is a reality."[269]

Fredi Baum, who served as interpreter at the fort, had been a Boy Scout in Yugoslavia. He was the guest of the Scout leaders of the Pontiac District during their gathering at St. Mary's Church. There, he witnessed the candlelight investiture service, an international Boy Scout ceremony, and remarked that the ceremony "had taken him back in memory some 13 years to the time when he was initiated." Baum gave those assembled a vivid account of a Scout hike he had participated in while mapping the contours of a mountain. There, he met with a serious accident that caused him to lose one of his legs. Due to the experience in first aid of the Scouts with him, Baum related, he was saved and brought home. Leaders of the Pontiac District expressed the hope that Baum would be able to visit the other training troops in the area.[270]

During the fall, with so many locals away in the service, local farmers experienced a serious shortage of workers to harvest the fruit crop. The situation was reaching crisis proportions, and farmers worried that the crop could go unharvested. One of the conditions of the refugees' placement at the fort was that they could not work for fear of being criticized for taking jobs away from American citizens. But due to this emergency situation, the War Refugee Board agreed to allow the refugees who were willing to work to harvest the local fruit crop. Their employment would be entirely voluntary, and prevailing wages would be paid.[271]

The volunteer call was very successful. Some 250 refugees at the fort expressed a willingness to work to harvest the fall crops. "There were indications that considerable assistance will be given fruit growers and farmers in the area by the war refugees," reported the *Palladium-Times*. The harvesting of pears, apples, potatoes, cabbage and other late crops would now take place, all of which required extra labor.[272]

Shelter residents began to form their own community within a community, setting up a companion advisory committee to work with the already established Oswego Advisory Committee. With donated equipment, shelter residents also began publishing their own weekly newspaper, the *Ontario Chronicle*. A full complement of classes began, including English instruction, shop classes, salon training and sewing. Shelter residents formed an orchestra, a chorus and a theater group, hosting shelter residents and Oswegonians at the fort theater.

As the Thanksgiving holiday approached, school programs were in full swing. The eighth graders at the Campus School voted for shelter resident Eric Levy to take the lead part of Miles Standish in their Thanksgiving play. "While the Oswego children in the Campus school have shown the friendliest feelings towards the children from the Fort," wrote *New York Post* reporter Naomi Jolles on a return visit to Oswego, "the same cannot be said for many of their parents....[The] president of the Board of Education regards the whole situation as having been forced upon the town. He expresses amazement at outsiders being interested in the project, saying, 'After all, it is only going to be a temporary thing.'...A Republican element in the town automatically opposes the Shelter as being another of 'that man' Roosevelt's doings." The teachers, however, according to Jolles, recognized in the presence of the refugee children as a real opportunity to teach democracy in action. "Says Marie Cullen, fifth grade teacher, 'Their being here brings a great deal we teach down to earth to our children.'"[273]

Though the town opinion on the presence of the refugees at the fort was divided and anxiety was beginning to build on the part of the refugees over their fate once the war ended, the spirit of the holiday season proved a good distraction for all.

As the holiday season approached, plans were formulated to celebrate the season at the shelter, the first time in many years the refugees would be able to engage in holiday preparations and celebration. The Oswego Advisory Committee contacted shelter director Joseph Smart about assisting with the observance of Christmas and the holiday season. "A Christmas tree on the fort parade grounds early on Christmas Eve to which the interested public from Oswego would be invited is under consideration," reported the *Palladium-Times*, "with the singing of carols by the massed church choirs of Oswego and by the refugee choir as special features. Mr. Smart reported that the refugee choral group will be heard in a Christmas Eve national radio broadcast singing carols in their native tongues."

Plans were already in progress for a nonsectarian Christmas Day service at the fort with representatives of the Catholic, Protestant and Jewish clergy of the city participating, the newspaper reported, as well as indoor

Santa (also known as John O'Connor of the Oswego Advisory Committee) distributes holiday gifts at the Fort Ontario Emergency Refugee Shelter. *Fort Ontario State Historic Site, New York State Office of Parks, Recreation, and Historic Preservation.*

Christmas programs for all the children of the refugees. The United Jewish Organization and the National YMCA would provide a gift for each child, and the gifts would be augmented with sweet treats provided by the people of Oswego.[274]

The *Ontario Chronicle* reported on the Chanukah festival planned for the residents of the shelter that included the distribution of 982 gifts so that every person would receive a parcel. In addition, children received toys in the synagogue. An artistic Chanukah event was planned in the post theater, with the shelter artists participating.[275]

In what was likely the best gift to shelter residents, the Oswego Advisory Committee recommended to Director Smart that restrictions to the number of passes for shelter residents to leave the fort grounds to visit the city be removed completely.[276]

M.J. Hoey of Oswego wrote of her encounter with one refugee mother and her young son while holiday shopping in Oswego in a letter to the "What People Say" column in the *Palladium-Times*. As she approached the counter to pay for her purchases, she observed a "very eager little boy" reaching for the toys displayed.

His whole body seemed to reach out in happiness. Then I realized this little lad had never even seen toys, much less owned any, until he came here. He had been in the grasp of a cruel war. He, at five, had been its victim, knowing its horrors, and its want....What a lesson I learned, as my only desire, up to then, was to make my purchases, go home to a cozy house, address Christmas cards, send gifts to children who have always known the joy of toys, the love of parents and plenty of food....Thank God for the refugees, all so smiling, happy, cheery, and happy to be in this blessed land. They have shown us much to be thankful for and also shown us to appreciate much that we have always taken for granted.[277]

Excitement also began to build for another national focus on the fort shelter. On December 23, 1944, at 4:00 p.m. the radio program "Christmas in Freedom" was broadcast to the nation, with noted journalist Dorothy Thompson as emcee from the NBC studios in New York City, and Joseph Smart, the shelter director, as the master of ceremonies from the fort.

"Every year we celebrate the birth of a child in Bethlehem, who was born in a stable because his mother would find no inn which would take her in," said Ms. Thompson.

We celebrate the birth of that refugee child with tinseled trees, carols, and orgies of spending on gifts, for in him we profess to see the light of the world and the hope of Mankind....It is told that at the birth of the babe of Bethlehem, that birth among cattle in a stall, angels appeared in the heavens promising a Peace on Earth to all men of good will. That Peace is not in the world, for Good Will is not in this world. Let us therefore be thankful that there is a little tiny piece of it in Oswego, New York.

"In Oswego," she related to her listeners, "around a thousand people are singing Christmas carols and rejoicing over the greatest boon that could possibly have befallen them. That boon is that they are in the United States where their lives have been saved."

"To those thousand, Oswego," she said, "is no small and confined place. It is the whole universe of human decency, good will, and freedom."

Fifteen-year-old Visko Marinkovicz, representing the young people of the shelter, and Margaret Weinstein, representing the adults of the shelter, spoke on behalf of shelter residents, thanking the country and the City of Oswego for the right to "live as men and not as hunted animals."[278]

The joy of the holiday season was touched by tragedy, however. Shelter resident Karoline Bleier had divorced her first husband, with whom she had two children before the war began. She remarried Geza Bleier, a Yugoslavian merchant. As a consequence of divorcing her first husband and marrying Geza, Karoline had to relinquish custody of her first two children while still in Europe. Eventually, Karoline and Geza had two children of their own: Ronald, born in 1942, and George, born in February 1944, just months before the family was chosen to be among the 982 refugees brought to the United States. Though she was relieved to be safe in the United States, Karoline was wracked with guilt over having to leave her two other children with their father in Europe.

Winter in Oswego can be notoriously harsh, and the winter of 1944–45 certainly lived up to that reputation. During the Christmas season, Ronald and George contracted whooping cough, and Karoline spent many sleepless nights nursing them back to health. Exhausted and still grieving the children she had left behind Karoline grew more and more depressed.[279]

Karoline Bleier was one of the students in Jessie Wood's English class at the shelter. In early November, Wood had her students write letters to her to practice writing in English. Karoline wrote about her husband and her two boys and ended with what may have been a prophetic statement about her state of mind. She wrote to Miss Wood, "I am tired because I have much to work in the house. Good bye, Karoline."[280]

On the night of December 18, Geza urged Karoline to attend a movie at the fort theater, believing this would be a good distraction for her after the exhaustion of caring for the young boys during their illness, wrote Ruth Gruber in her memoir, *Haven.*

> *Karoline protested she was too tired for the movie, but Geza persisted, and Karoline left the barracks to go to the movie.*
>
> *The camp was already covered with snow, but soon the winds off Lake Ontario whipped up another blizzard,*
>
> *When neighbors began returning from the movie, Geza asked them if they had seen Karoline, but no one reported seeing her.*
>
> *Hours drifted by and still Karoline did not come back. Geza called the camp police, and they searched, digging through ten foot high drifts. Other people joined the search while 50 mile per hour winds roared off the lake....Early in the morning of December 19 the search party found Karoline on the banks of the Barge Canal.*

The entry about her in the Riverside Cemetery book says she died from acute poisoning, an autopsy later revealing she had swallowed [a great quantity of] *aspirin tablets.*[281]

Karoline's death cast a long shadow over the holiday spirit of the camp. Her funeral took place on the last day of 1944 at the Riverside Cemetery, just a few miles from Fort Ontario. A great number of her friends, as well as Mr. and Mrs. Joseph Smart, were in attendance. In the days and weeks that followed, several women from the shelter stepped in to assist Geza with the care of his two young boys.[282]

THE NEW YEAR DAWNED cold and gray along the shores of Lake Ontario. The holiday season past, a daily routine settled in once again over the shelter. The war was still raging in Europe and in the Pacific, but Allied forces were gaining ground. There was hope that 1945 would see an end to the world conflicts. Adults at the shelter became more anxious about what their next steps would be once the war ended. Many hoped they would be allowed to stay in the United States despite the declaration form they'd signed agreeing to return to their homelands at war's end.

The city's residents were used to seeing the people from the shelter in town patronizing local businesses, but during the start of the new year, this gave rise to a perception on the part of some local people that the refugees were purchasing luxury items with their government allowances instead of basic supplies. Director Smart encouraged the refugees to invest any surplus funds in American war bonds, demonstrating their appreciation for the United States and, in turn, countering any negative public opinion.[283]

A report in the *Palladium-Times* in January announced that the small amounts of money the refugees brought with them from Italy and held by the Allied Control Commission were being returned. "Practically all the refugees want to conserve their small funds for the time when they will make their adjustment back to normal life and, for practically all, the savings will be in the form of war bonds." The report continued, "This is not the first time the refugees have shown their desire to sacrifice in every way possible for the war effort," citing an earlier benefit event put on by shelter residents that raised "a sizable fund for the National Red Cross."[284]

The early part of 1945 at the shelter was marked again by tragedy. Arpad Buchler, forty-two, of Yugoslavia, was smothered to death in mid-February when a large coal pile he was shoveling collapsed, burying him beneath it. Despite frantic efforts to free Buchler, he died before he could be released.[285]

Long winter days, uncertainty about their fate, the tragic loss of two shelter residents and the inability of the refugees to move very far beyond the confines of the fort and Oswego gave rise to a growing discontent on the part of many.

PM newspaper reporter Eleanor Morehead described the refugees' mindset in a story in the February 25 edition. "Physically they are in the U.S.A. In every other sense they live in a never-never land with no past, apparently no future, and only a painful present….Persons young and old, men and women, who came here filled with hope for a new and better future in a land which at last they could call home, leaving their past behind in Europe [are] now marking time helplessly as the days and months pass, that hope is fast fading; they live today in constant dread of an unknown future day when the war will end, and they will be sent back…to what?"[286]

New York Post reporter Naomi Jolles returned to the shelter in March and observed the mood shift that had taken place among the refugees. "All through the camp is the whispered hope that somehow a way may be found to settle permanently in this country." Jolles noted, "The chance to come to the U.S. through President Roosevelt's order took people out of the path of war. At the same time, it has placed them apart from life." Shelter resident Margaret Ehremstamm spoke with Jolles and remarked, "Now that things are better, we seem to show less patience. When it was harder, we just had to hold on to keep going. But here everything is so close. Just outside the gate."[287]

While the shelter's adult residents worried, the shelter's young people were embracing American life, culture and history as students in Oswego's schools. Steffi Steinberg, along with the other Oswego High School students from the shelter, were focused on the Constitution during Bill of Rights week. An essay by Steinberg was the subject of a news report in the *Palladium-Times*. "Out of the discussions and writings came the voice of the refugee students speaking about the priceless value of human rights in America. In contrast to Americans who have always taken their rights for granted is added the thoughts of one refugee who has been denied her rights in her native land."

Steinberg wrote, "The fact I admire most is the great unity among a people living on such a great continent peacefully together….America since 1787 is bound together by its Constitution which every American, great and small, bears in his heart as the greatest power—the supreme law of his country. It is that which everybody, rich and poor, old and young, possesses and that nobody can take away from him."[288]

Though Steffi Steinberg and others at the shelter longed to be part of that American democracy, it would be months before a decision was reached on the fate of the refugees.

On April 12, 1945, President Franklin Roosevelt, the man who exercised his power to bring them to safety and security in the United States at Fort Ontario, died in Warm Springs, Georgia. Immediately after his passing, American democracy continued under the presidency of Roosevelt's vice president, Harry Truman.

The mood at the shelter in mid-April upon learning of the passing of the man many considered their savior was somber. The shelter residents grew ever more anxious, speculating about how the new president would view their status.

The *Ontario Chronicle* printed copies of three telegrams sent by the fort refugees on Roosevelt's passing, expressing their deepest sympathies at the loss of the president. The telegrams were sent to President Truman, Mrs. Eleanor Roosevelt and Mr. Harold Ickes, and they noted that the refugees joined others in the nation mourning "the death of a great man who fought for and defended the rights of liberty and freedom."[289]

On May 8, 1945, Germany unconditionally surrendered its military forces to the Allies, including the United States. Celebrations erupted around the world. For residents of the Fort Ontario Emergency Refugee Shelter, the news brought intense speculation about what would happen to them now that war in Europe had ended. Rumors ran rampant throughout the shelter population, and discussions about their fate were once again the focus of the media.

Just before the official end of the war in Europe was announced, a familiar face and staunch supporter of the refugees, shelter director Joseph Smart, announced his decision to leave his post as director. Smart's decision was motivated by rumors that a ship had already been chartered to take the fort refugees back to Europe. In an interview years later, Smart explained what prompted his decision to resign and lead a national effort to convince officials of the federal government to allow the refugees who wished to remain in the country to do so.

Smart said when he confronted his Washington, D.C. boss, Dillon Myer, he was told that a final decision had been made about the refugees and that they were indeed to be sent back to Europe. A group of shelter residents became aware that they were going to be required to return to Europe and went to Smart asking if an outside committee of prominent people could be organized to plead their case before the American public, Congress and the president. The consensus was that if anyone could effectively organize this effort, it was Smart himself who had the experience with the shelter population and who understood their problem better than anyone else. Smart agreed to lead the effort, and to do so, he resigned from his position in mid-May.[290]

Smart worked quickly to line up support, forming the Friends of Fort Ontario Guest Refugees Committee and opening an office for the committee in New York City. A host of notable national figures signed on to Smart's committee, as did every member of the Oswego Advisory Committee. The Oswego contingent joined notables from across the United States, including Albert Einstein; Eleanor Roosevelt; journalist and writer Katherine Anne Porter; the founder of public relations, Edward Bernays; former New York governor Herbert Lehman; singer and actress Sophie Tucker; and Nobel Prize winner Thomas Mann, among many others.[291]

Smart's national group was formed on the heels of an effort by the Oswego Advisory Committee, which, in mid-May, drafted and sent to officials in Washington, D.C., a document titled "A Memorial to the President and the Congress of the United States Concerning the Freedom of War Refugees Temporarily Living at Fort Ontario, Oswego, New York." The "Memorial" pleaded the case to allow the refugees to remain in the United States.

It read in part:

> *These refugees have now lived in our land for almost a year. They have a tentative security, the friendship of the people of Oswego whom they have been able to meet, modest provision for food, shelter, and medical care. But instead of the freedom they sought and of which they dreamed, they have been closely held in a fenced area on the shores of Lake Ontario, with permission to be absent from the camp for only six-hour periods, and without permission to visit relatives or friends beyond the limits of the city of Oswego. Instead of the opportunity to fashion a new life for themselves and their families, they have been deprived of a chance to work at any gainful or life building pursuits, and this last in the face of a local and national war manpower shortage of critical proportions.... When, for so long, one's very life has been in jeopardy, all the ramifications of a document one signs to gain security do not immediately become evident, and it does not seem fair to enforce commitments which are inhumane and which are accepted only in desperation....Regardless of what they signed, they cannot all go back to their homelands, for in some cases these have been destroyed; and approximately one-third have been deprived of citizenship in the countries*

- 5 -

or private agencies are ready to care for them, if necessary, and guarantee that they shall not become public charges.

II. In this period of critical manpower shortage, the refugees should be permitted to accept gainful employment, and build themselves anew into their professions. In the case of many who have seen their productive years uselessly spent and no security ahead for their families, this is an imperative need.

III. The refugees who would, except for their present peculiar circumstances, be eligible under our existing immigration quotas should be permitted, should they so desire, to become citizens of the United States under existing rules and regulations.

IV. Those who desire to return to their homeland or any portion of the world should be given the opportunity as soon as conditions permit.

Finally, the Committee believes that the problem of these 982 refugees now living at Fort Ontario, should be considered unique and apart from all other refugees problems consequent to the present war. They constitute our country's immediate responsibility. It is the nation's clear duty, in charity and decency, to carry to its logical solution this definite obligation.

The memorial signed by members of the Oswego Advisory Committee. *Oswego County Historical Society.*

of their origin.…Unless we are to deny the very essence of what we are fighting for now and have always stood for (life, liberty and the pursuit of happiness), we should give our guests their freedom.[292]

The document was signed by twenty-seven Oswego citizens representing a cross-section of the town, including businessmen, educators, clergy, union representatives and members of local fraternal and service organizations. These were the people who had come to know the shelter residents best, and they represented the loudest voices among a growing chorus declaring that the 982 people of the Fort Ontario Emergency Refugee Shelter should be allowed to remain in the United States.

Six Months in Limbo

Joseph Smart and the Oswego Citizens Advisory Committee, along with many others, worked through the summer and fall of 1945 to plead the case for the refugees. The end of June brought members of a subcommittee of the House of Representatives Committee on Immigration and Naturalization to Oswego for a two-day hearing at Fort Ontario. The committee chair, Representative Samuel Dickstein of New York, scheduled the hearings for June 25 and 26. But trouble began to brew in advance of those hearings.

On May 18, the *Palladium-Times* reported the results of a survey that showed a large majority of shelter residents wished to remain in the United States.

> While a majority of the refugees are desirous of remaining in the United States, there are some who are anxious to gain admission to other countries to establish their future homes....Because of the fact that 641 have expressed their hope of remaining in the United States to be legally admitted under existing immigration quotas, an Immigration Sub-committee of the House of Representatives has announced that it will begin hearings [in June] with a view of determining the future of shelter residents.[293]

The frustration that had been growing on the part of shelter residents about their fate finally arrived on the pages of the *Palladium-Times* in the form of a letter to the "What People Say" column penned by shelter resident

Shelter artist Max
Sipser expresses the
frustration of the
refugees awaiting
a determination
about their status.
Ontario Chronicle,
*Special Collections,
Penfield Library, State
University of New York
at Oswego.*

Bernard Guillemin. The lengthy letter acknowledged that the refugees had
signed a declaration promising to return to their homelands before boarding
the ship in Italy. However, he noted that confusion and misinterpretation
over what the declaration really meant left many of the 982 with the hope
and expectation that at war's end, they would be admitted to the United
States if they so desired. Speaking of their confinement since August 1944
he said:

> *When we accepted the invitation of the American government in Italy, we
> could not imagine that many people in the best 4 years of manhood, fit and
> hungry for work, "guests" in the United States, would be condemned to
> remain in a place which presents an unhealthy mixture of an old people's
> home and a kindergarten. Still less we imagined that 1,000 people, unrelated
> to each other and only assembled by accident, would be condemned in the
> freest country of the world to live in a ghetto which is humiliating and
> injurious both for the Jewish and Christian residents.*

Guillemin acknowledged the "immense contribution" of the American fighting forces to victory over tyranny and expressed the desire to now become part of America as well. "Those of us who are young and feel a natural desire for action will not appreciate American hospitality as long as they are secluded and separated from America itself, the object of their admiration." The confinement of the refugees to the fort and the city of Oswego, declared Guillemin, "is a painful fact that men who as friends and admirers of America and with faith in American freedom, American generosity and the practical mind of the American people accepted the invitation of President Roosevelt [but] have been for nine months imprisoned at Fort Ontario."[294]

The Guillemin letter set off a firestorm of debate, bringing heretofore private grumblings about the presence of the refugees in the community to the public sphere. It brought fervent support for the presence of the refugees as well. True to his word, publisher Edwin Waterbury and his "What People Say" column provided the forum for all these sentiments to be publicly expressed.

F. Charles McCarthy of Syracuse was outraged at the Guillemin letter, calling for a Congressional investigation. "In [Guillemin's] statement the American people stand accused of maintaining a sort of prison camp, whereas it was thought by the refugees they were to enjoy all the rights and privileges of American citizens." McCarthy noted that Guillemin may not be speaking for all the refugees at the fort but sounded an alarm about their already shaky status. "In light of the charges set forth it becomes not merely a local but a national issue and should be recognized as such by Washington. If there were secret documents entering into the refugee case not in accordance with American traditions, the whole country should know about them."

Robert Newstead of Oswego, who had a son fighting in the Pacific theater, concurred with McCarthy. "I have a son. He and his buddies are fighting… eating K-rations and liking it; they are crawling in dirt and filth on the other side of the world. Blood, sweat, and stubble covers their faces.…They have no time to stop and complain of what they want or haven't got. They are fighting for the same liberty you have and are complaining about."

In the same column, William T. Griffiths of Oswego expressed support for the refugees, asking why the United States would send them "back to the countries from whence they came in order that they may live and work alongside the very people who murdered their relatives and friends?"[295]

Concern immediately grew among shelter residents that Guillemin's letter might jeopardize any goodwill that had thus far been generated about allowing them to remain in the United States. To that end, shelter residents went to the pages of the "What People Say" column to counter what Guillemin had said.

Arthur Hirt and Ernest Flatau, writing on behalf of a meeting of the shelter refugees to respond to the Guillemin letter, stated that the letter had "produced such a profound excitement among the Shelter residents that they had reunited in a community meeting…in order to express their resentment against this tactless and thoughtless declaration." They declared that Guillemin did not have authority to speak on anyone's behalf but his own. Shelter residents did not authorize his statement and do not agree with it. In addition, they expressed appreciation for everything offered to them by the American government and the American people. "The shelter residents regret the incident. They are convinced that the fairness of the American people is giving them full guarantee that the responsibility for a statement of a single person will not be burdened on the entire Fort Ontario community."

In the same column, Robert Brewer of Oswego expressed support for the refugees, saying he had become acquainted with a number of them, first through the fence and later in their homes, as well as his own. "It is true that almost every refugee hopes to be permitted to remain in the U.S.A. and to eventually become a citizen. It is also true that the restrictions, although probably necessary, also are irksome. It is also true that after five years of 'marking time' in their professions and lives, these people are impatient to start progressing again.…But for all these truths, all of the refugees whom I know quietly express their hopes…with no thought of insisting or criticizing." Brewer concluded by suggesting that "any of our national senators or representatives who can, should, without announcement or fanfare, visit incognito some of the homes at the shelter to get first-hand information to present to Congress in the near future."[296]

Newstead followed up with a second critical letter published in the "What People Say" column in early June, charging that the Oswego Advisory Committee was attempting to propagandize local citizens. He wrote that the committee members "had the nerve and audacity to write that their plea on behalf of the refugees [the Memorial sent to the President and to Congress] is in conformity with the thinking of the citizens of Oswego. How little they know about the thinking of our citizens to make a statement like that.…I think," he concluded, "we might more wisely devote our time in remembering that our sons and daughters overseas have and deserve a far greater claim on our services than a group of people who seem to be plentifully supplied with money if not with sympathy."[297]

E. Charles McCarthy sent a follow-up letter to the "What People Say" column as well. On June 23, he, too, mentioned the "great amount of propaganda being spread before the public concerning the…refugees" and said, "This propaganda bears all the earmarks of the lobbying tactics used so frequently in forcing through measures injurious to public interests." He asked, "Has it come to pass that our conquering heroes will be obliged to secure lobbyists in order to obtain the rights and privileges they so richly deserve? I would like very much to get in touch through correspondence with unemployed soldiers whose talents are not being publicized. Perhaps some plan might be formulated," McCarthy suggested, "to do for Americans what some folks are trying to do for foreigners."[298]

AGAINST THIS BACKDROP, CONGRESSMAN Samuel Dickstein opened the hearing into the status of the fort refugees on Monday, June 25. It was covered by many local and national news outlets. The *Syracuse Herald Journal* called the hearings "democracy in action" and suggested that the hearings will be "watched throughout the country and in other lands." The *Herald* noted that the attorney general's office in Washington had ruled the refugees must be deported but that citizens "of Syracuse and of other places have expressed themselves in sympathy with these people and against their return to Europe."[299]

Dickstein and the five members of his subcommittee heard two days of testimony from shelter residents and community members. Introducing the situation at the Fort Ontario Emergency Refugee Shelter to the congressmen were Edward B. Marks Jr. of the War Relocation Authority and Brigadier General William O'Dwyer of the president's War Refugee Board. They were followed by fourteen members of the Fort Ontario Shelter Boy Scout troop.

In his testimony, Marks related that the wording of the order by which the refugees were brought to the United States, "under appropriate security restrictions," had been an issue from the beginning, because "it did mean a kind of indeterminate sentence. It has not been possible for them to leave the Fort and join, or even visit their relatives and friends throughout the country." Marks added that with the war ended in Europe, a small number of the refugees were able to return to Yugoslavia and opted to do so. But the problem "we have here," he said, is that "there are a large number of people at the shelter who have no real homeland, so to speak, to return to. At least they feel that way." He also noted that thirty-four heads of families at the shelter have a total of forty immediate relatives currently serving in the United States armed forces.

Marks was followed by General O'Dwyer, who discussed the issue of returning the refugees to their homelands as well.

> *The largest single category of refugees at Oswego are "stateless" Jews originating in Austria, Germany, and Balkan countries. The problem of these people, and perhaps of the "stateless" Poles, is far from an ultimate solution. Under present physical, psychological, and political conditions they have no homeland to which to return....In my opinion it would not be in accordance with the late President's commitment, and our government's political and humanitarian policies, to return "stateless" Jews arbitrarily to Germany and Austria, or unwilling nationals to the countries of their citizenship.*

O'Dwyer gave extensive testimony on the overwhelmingly challenging conditions in Europe regarding "stateless" peoples. By comparison, he said, this very small group at the only shelter in the United States could be easily assimilated into the country without undue burden and without opening the floodgates to unlimited immigration. O'Dwyer outlined the complex set of circumstances, mostly political in nature, that were conspiring to prevent a timely resolution for the fort refugees. He provided options for solutions to the problem for the subcommittee to consider.

The full transcript of the subcommittee hearings, in particular, General O'Dwyer's testimony, indicated a willingness, at least on the part of Congressman Dickstein, to find a way to allow the refugees to stay. Subcommittee members were impressed with the testimony of the fort Boy Scouts and the many shelter residents, young and old, who were questioned by the committee members. Joining the appeal to the Dickstein subcommittee were officials of the shelter, including, in addition to Edward Marks, Malcolm Pitts, the current shelter director, and Ruth Gruber.

The second day of the hearings focused on the educators who had interacted with the refugees in the elementary schools, the high school and at the college. Testimony was given by Ralph Swetman of the Oswego State Teachers College; Charles Riley, the superintendent of the Oswego schools; Virginia Dean, the principal of Fitzhugh Park School; Susan Donovan, the principal of School No. 2; Ralph Faust, the principal of Oswego High School; Charles Wells, a professor at State Teachers College; Paul Alfred, the vice-principal of Fitzhugh Park School; Marion Mahar, a professor at

Oswego State Teachers College; Harold Alford of Oswego State Teachers College; and Eric Brunger of Campus Elementary School.[300]

Typical of the remarks on the part of the city's educators were those expressed by Superintendent Charles Riley, which were reported in the *Palladium-Times*. "[Riley] said he had carefully studied the refugee students and pupils and that their scholastic achievement was really amazing. If permitted to remain here two or three years, they will develop into outstanding pupils and students. Mr. Riley said he believed they should not be discriminated against and if they are to be sent back to Europe it would amount to just that."

Harry Mizen and Edwin Waterbury of the Oswego Advisory Committee were then questioned by committee members, as was Thomas Mowatt, the chief of police of the City of Oswego. Each testified about the positive experiences they'd had with the shelter residents since their arrival nearly a year before. Mowatt said he was not aware of any incidents requiring police intervention in the city, and he reported that local businesspeople who regularly interacted with the shelter residents reported very favorably on those interactions. Eighteen additional shelter residents were questioned by members of the Dickstein subcommittee on the second day as well.

Shelter resident Ernest Braun was asked about a medical preparation he had invented that cured certain skin diseases and also depilated the skin around wounded skin surfaces. Braun explained that the current practice in hospitals in the United States and abroad to prevent wound infection, for example, on the hand was to remove the hairs on the skin to better view the wound and prevent infection. In some cases, said Braun, the removal must be done by pulling out one hair at a time, a painful procedure. Instead, he said, "I take my preparation, and put it on the wounded surface and it doesn't make any irritation on the skin, and you wash it off and the hand is clean, and it doesn't burn."

Braun related that the preparation he'd invented was first tested in a hospital in Treviso and that the Italian government began to use it in their hospitals. However, once the Germans entered Italy, Braun was forced to go into hiding. "I was protected by a priest of the Vatican, who gave me permission to enter into the Library of the Vatican, where I could do my research work. They gave me papers where I was no longer Ernest Braun, but Enrico Bianci."

Once Rome was liberated by the Americans, Braun said he was introduced to the chief of the American public health and welfare service, and Braun's preparation was examined by the American medical staff there. "They said that they would need it badly for the hospitals all over the United States, and when I finished my experiment [the chief] said he would do everything possible to send me to America." A few weeks later, Braun was part of the 982 headed to the United States and Fort Ontario, where he continued his research.[301]

A story in the Upstate University Hospital newsletter reported on Braun's presentation to physicians at the medical school there.

> *During his 18-month stay in the Oswego fort, Braun continued to develop medicinal skin ointments he had been working on in Europe. In Oswego, Braun applied for a patent and wrote letters to the U.S. Attorney General and others in Washington, DC. After a year of research and letter writing, Braun was invited to Syracuse University to present his work to Dr. Weiskotten, Dr. Hiss and colleagues at the medical school.*
>
> *"I was finally given the opportunity to exhibit the properties of my preparations," Braun later wrote about his meeting with the faculty. "The experiments were successful, and I was advised…to produce the [skin ointments] so that the Army and Navy [could] make use of them. They cure certain skin diseases…due to infection and inflammation." Despite enormous obstacles, Braun had created a medical compound that would revolutionize presurgical wound care.*[302]

Dickstein questioned Braun about the status of Braun's research and the use of his medical compound. Braun said he had a patent pending with the Patent Office in Washington. "Did you offer that preparation to the American government?" Dickstein asked. Braun responded that he had presented the whole preparation, free of charge, to the American hospitals.[303]

Other shelter residents told the stories of their experiences in Europe to the congressmen, including Matilda Nitsch, who had assisted in the escape of more than five hundred people from the Nazis and who now expressed her desire to remain in the United States.

Peter Ouroussoff, a former Russian businessman, was asked about a document that listed him as a Russian prince. Dickstein asked if Ouroussoff would be willing to give up that title for American citizenship. "Most certainly," answered Ouroussoff. "On the paper, I put my father, I mentioned that my father was a prince; I didn't mention it for me personally, but no doubt, I am perfectly willing to give it up." To this, Dickstein replied, "It isn't worth much anyway." "No," said Ouroussoff. "It is a thing of the past."

Many of the shelter residents who testified listed relatives already in the country with whom they could live, and many had family in the United States armed services. Their stories of flight and survival were dramatic. Most had spent time in German concentration camps. Many, like Dr. Ernst Flatau, had nearly completed the process to immigrate to the United States when the outbreak of war dashed those plans. Flatau also addressed the document the refugees had signed agreeing to return to Europe after the war and the confusion surrounding the signing. "It was almost impossible to read, because of the small tables, and so many people," he said. People were hanging over each other, anxious to sign the paperwork for a chance to be admitted to the United States.

When Flatau was asked, if had he known the full circumstances of the situation at Fort Ontario, would he have signed the document or preferred to stay in Italy, Flatau responded, "I would have signed in every way." Ironically, as the committee members learned, Flatau's mother and grandfather were both American citizens. His mother had lost her American citizenship by marriage but regained it under the American laws then in place after the death of her husband.

In another irony, shelter resident Dr. Ernst Wolff, a novelist and screenwriter before the Nazis marched in, informed committee members that he had been in the United States in Hollywood twenty years before, selling a novel he'd written. Wolff had previously written sixty novels that sold three million copies. Like Dr. Flatau, Wolff was about to complete the process to immigrate when the American consulate in Rome closed.

Congressman John Lesinski from Michigan had been busy outside the fort hearing room, interviewing others who were not on the list of those scheduled to testify. He reported his findings to fellow committee members once he was back in the hearing room. "I have interviewed some people outside, and I had about 20 out there. They have told me a very sad story of how they have traveled and escaped from country to country for the last 6 years, and they naturally would sign any type of paper as long as they could come to America.…So when it gets down to the fundamental part of all their stories, you will find that every immigrant here is in the same position; they actually have no country to go back to."[304]

At the close of the hearings, Chairman Dickstein outlined three issues to be decided with regard to the refugees. One: Should they be released as individuals on their own recognizance? Two: Should they be released as individuals on bonds which might necessitate a cost of more than $1 million? Three, and Dickstein said this was the option he preferred: Should the refugees be declared immigrants here illegally? In such case, they would be directly under the control of immigration authorities and could be given pre-examination, and then they would be taken to Canada, which would accept them under that status. Those entitled to entrance back to the United States under quota of their countries of origin would then be able to apply for visas to legally enter the United States. Dickstein said he hoped to have a report on the hearings and the recommendations before Congress adjourned.[305]

For the shelter's young people, the summer of 1945 was marked by celebration, as six residents graduated with the class of '45 from the Oswego High School. They would also enjoy a typical American summer camp experience, thanks to the arrival of Esther Morrison and eleven other members of a Quaker-sponsored team, who would teach Native crafts, lead hikes, organize picnics and present shows and songfests.

While the young people of the shelter enjoyed a carefree summer, the adults experienced continued anxiety about their eventual fate. Though the Dickstein hearings raised their hopes for a speedy solution, those hopes were dashed on July 6, when the full House Immigration and Naturalization Committee rejected the resolution of the Dickstein subcommittee that would have allowed the refugees to leave the fort and enter America. Instead, the full committee voted that the Departments of State and Justice, not Congress, "should ascertain the practicability of returning the refugees to their homelands." If that was not practical, the full committee suggested, the Attorney General should declare the Fort refugees illegally present in the country and commence deportation proceedings. They were now in even greater danger of being sent back to Europe.[306]

Continued uncertainty about whether the fort refugees would be allowed to stay in the United States or sent back to Europe fueled more letters to the "What People Say" column during July and August.

Thelma Mason of Mexico, New York, had a son in the service. She said she worked a week at the shelter but then resigned after witnessing "good, young, able-bodied people lying around in the shade. Could a farmer, much as they need help, hire one?" she asked. "No, they are guests of the U.S....I am not the only mother of service boys who resent them here." She went on to suggest that "Mrs. Roosevelt…purchase an island someplace and take them all on it and she herself personally oversee them."[307]

Ardella Parkhurst of Oswego followed with her critique of the refugees on July 26, accusing one of following her when she was shopping in the city. She complained about shortages of items, such as shoes and ice cream, and said it was because these items were all going to the people at the fort. "When our boys come home from overseas, they want the good old Oswego they left," she declared. "They don't want it the way the future looks now."[308]

The Parkhurst letter brought a flurry of replies in the pages of the *Palladium-Times* from those who agreed with her and those who did not. Shelter resident Richard Arvay suggested, "If Mrs. Parkhurst had experienced only a part of the suffering, starvation, and sorrow that lies behind each of us, she would be ashamed to think such thoughts."[309] Writer Marie Girmant of Oswego echoed Arvay's sentiment. "To anyone unduly concerned about the refugees," she said, "give thought to the Golden Rule, that you are your brother's keeper and that but for the grace of God you too might be a refugee."[310]

Perhaps the most eloquent defense of the refugees came on July 30 in a letter penned by Tec 5 Fred Bohm, 104th Division, whose parents were living at the fort shelter. "I came here…after having fought through the winter and spring campaign in Holland and Germany where I was wounded. I am going to be deployed to the Pacific.…I express my disgust and my shame, not only on my personal behalf, but also on behalf of many other American boys who fought in Europe and whose fathers and mothers are refugees at Fort Ontario." Bohm reminded readers that the refugees did want to work to help local farmers and others, but except for a short period when they helped harvest the fruit crop in the fall, they were not allowed to work at jobs in the United States.

And Bohm was well-acquainted with the enormous problem of stateless people in Europe, having just witnessed it firsthand. Thousands of refugees, said Bohm, are sheltering in Italy and France "and other destroyed and ruined countries." By contrast, he continued, the fort refugees represented "less than a drop of water in the ocean," and he wondered if Mrs. Parkhurst, after his statement of facts about the dire situation for stateless people in Europe, might reconsider and express her regrets in the paper.[311]

Letters to the "What People Say" column continued to appear in the August editions of the *Palladium-Times*, reacting to Mrs. Parkhurst's letter. Kathleen Roberts of Oswego remarked:

> *How easy it is to forget that our own forefathers were also refugees, were also discriminated against.…There is a great deal of evidence on both sides of this controversy, and the conduct of both sides is somewhat open to censure, but this question can never be settled by the backyard bickerings*

which have taken place over our fences. Whether these people stay in our country or not. Whether they are Jewish or Gentile. Whether or not they speak English is not entirely pertinent. The real problem, simply stated, is this: They are human beings and our neighbors and as such are deserving of humane treatment....I appeal to my fellow townsmen for a more tolerant attitude toward them for the duration of their visit here.[312]

She was joined in an appeal for tolerance by Private Arthur F. Kelly of Oswego, who served with the parachute infantry. He was an ex–prisoner of war who was home on leave. Kelly expressed surprise and disappointment at the tone of the letters in the newspaper.

These people have suffered in a way that home front Americans know nothing whatever about. I know. I witnessed the devastation administered to the blood-stained battlefields of Europe. These people once occupied the battlefields. They have been through a great deal of suffering and heartache....I can't blame them for wanting to stay in this wonderful land of ours, but I do feel that they should return to their homelands and try to use the experiences gained in America for the rebuilding of their lands and governments.[313]

Despite the pleas of Roberts and Kelly for tolerance, the critical letters continued into August. By late fall, however, the "What People Say" column letters refocused on local politics and the mayoral race in Oswego, among other topics. As 1945 drew to a close and another harsh winter approached, the fate of the fort refugees remained undecided by the political powers in Washington. With no end to their confinement in sight, the writers, musicians and performers among the shelter population moved their plea for freedom from the pages of the newspaper to the pages of a musical score.

THE GOLDEN CAGE AND THOSE WHO REMAINED

Charles Abeles, an Austrian composer, conductor and pianist, said his first aim, on arrival at the Fort Ontario Emergency Refugee Shelter, was to organize a musical life there. He felt music would help overcome the daily preoccupations and sorrows of his fellow shelter residents. To that end, Abeles founded the Ontario Orchestra with himself as the conductor.[314]

Music was Abeles's savior while he was fleeing Nazi persecution in war-torn Europe. As a young person, he exhibited exceptional musical talent and made a living before the war as a musician in Baden and Vienna, with a repertoire of operetta hits, waltzes, Viennese songs and his own compositions. He married a Catholic seamstress and continued his career until Austria was annexed to the German Reich. This ended his employment, and like so many Jews, Charles was taken into custody then sent to the Dachau Concentration Camp. His Catholic wife managed to get him released, and they escaped to Italy. There, he was interned as well, but music saved him from the fate that befell so many others. In Dachau, he had to play for the guards. In Italy, he gave piano lessons outside the camp and took part in high-level cultural programs. When the opportunity to come to the United States was presented in the summer of 1944, Charles boarded the *Henry Gibbins* and was among the 982 refugees who settled at Fort Ontario.

"While Charly was still 'rather depressed and exhausted' when he was admitted to the camp, his condition changed very quickly when he was given the opportunity to develop and implement a music program for the camp," said his nephew Peter Koppitz in a remembrance titled *Charles Abeles' Survival in Italy.*

He dedicated himself to this task with enthusiasm, gave music lessons to children and young people, founded an orchestra, and created discussion groups that listened to music together. He accompanied singers and soloists at their performances and even played at all festivals in the camp without getting tired until late at night. Not enough with that, he now composed tirelessly. Compositions were written to thank the captain [of the Henry Gibbins], *Ruth Gruber, who had tirelessly looked after the refugees, and the camp manager. The operettas* The King's Daughter, A Hen Party in Florida *and* The Golden Cage *were all written in 1944 and were performed at the camp to great acclaim. Trained musicians, singers, ballet dancers all jumped at the opportunities these performances offered them. They strengthened the courage of all participants and all spectators.*[315]

Music proved to be particularly needed in the waning days of 1945. "As they awaited the Christmas holiday season most of the shelter residents were discouraged by the seeming fruitlessness of their own efforts and the attempts of their relatives and friends and interested committees to obtain their freedom," recalled Edward Marks in *Token Shipment: The Story of America's Refugee Shelter*. "They had seen two Government deputations, one Congressional and one administrative, make exhaustive inquiries into the shelter problem without attaining any visible result." Despairing of an early resolution of their status, they were resigned to yet another winter along the shores of Lake Ontario.[316]

In November, Abeles, along with artist and writer Miriam Sommerburg, wrote the operetta *The Golden Cage*, the golden cage being a metaphor for the fort shelter, where all their physical needs were met but they lacked freedom, the one thing they most desired. The plot unfolded their story from life in Europe to the voyage to America and their experiences at the shelter.

Months earlier, the *Ontario Chronicle* had sponsored an essay contest for shelter residents, and seventeen-year-old Adam Munz won first prize. His essay perhaps presaged Abeles's and Sommerburg's operetta when he described the plight of the young people at the shelter. Referring to conversations with fellow shelter residents, he wrote, in part:

As we talked…among us…we came to the conclusion that really nothing can satisfy our youth here at the Fort.…Let us take the example of a small little bird which you take and put up in a nice comfortable cage. You take well care of the bird; you give him his daily food; you give him some sugar from time to time. Then, after a few weeks when he is well-acquainted to the room he is in, you close the window and let him spread his wings between the four walls. The little bird will like it at the beginning; but later he will look with a sad eye through the glass when he sees his fellows enjoy liberty! You will be surprised when a few years later your little bird will die. He will die because he is thirsty, thirsty for liberty he cannot enjoy. So is every single being in the world.[317]

On December 22, just before the operetta *The Golden Cage* by Abeles and Sommerburg was set to be performed, President Harry Truman, the man who famously displayed a sign reading "The Buck Stops Here" in the Oval Office, took the matter of the Fort Ontario refugees in his own hands. "In a statement...the President included the Fort Ontario refugees in the order under which...European refugees would be permitted to enter the U.S. annually under national quotas," reported the *Palladium-Times*.[318]

The news was greeted with immense relief and joy by the shelter residents. Truman had given the refugees the best Christmas gift of all, their freedom, and a new finale was written for *The Golden Cage* operetta. The show debuted on New Year's Eve 1945, with a grand celebration following the performance. Though no program for the performance was ever found, it is likely that Leo Mirkovic, the Yugoslavian singer who had been the leading baritone of the Yugoslav National Opera before he was forced to flee from the Nazis, and Manya Hartmayer-Breuer, the Polish singer who was so talented that she was released from one concentration camp due to her beautiful singing voice, had leading parts.[319]

After a joyous holiday season, shelter residents prepared to leave the fort and begin their lives again, this time in the United States. They had entered the United States as "guests" of the president and the American government, so there needed to be a process by which they could enter again to declare their desire for citizenship. The solution came from the Canadian government, which accepted the fort refugees at Niagara Falls, across the Rainbow Bridge from the United States. It was just a few hours' drive from Oswego. Shelter residents boarded buses in the early part of February and left the country for Canada. There, they were quickly processed by immigration officials, given visas and were then able to return to the United States. From there, they dispersed across the country, some joining family or friends already awaiting their arrival. Some selected major cities on the East Coast, including New York City, Philadelphia and Baltimore.

The refugees' eighteen-month residence in Oswego, New York, was now a part of their history, but many of the friendships they had forged with

After eighteen months of internment, the refugees were allowed to leave Oswego. Because they had come into the country outside the immigration laws, they had to travel to Canada first to get the proper visas to enter the United States as legal immigrants. Groups of shelter residents are pictured waiting to board the buses at the fort barracks. *National Archives.*

Oswegonians continued through letters and visits over the ensuing years. For their part, Oswegonians, with their veterans now home from the war, worked to re-establish normal lives, now safe from the threat of war. The fort reverted to New York State ownership in April 1946. The New York State Housing Authority then converted it to a housing complex to provide affordable housing for returning veterans. It opened as a State Historic Site in the early 1950s and was added to the National Register of Historic Places on December 18, 1970. It continues to operate as a New York State Park.

THOUGH MOST OF THE residents of the shelter moved away, three families, the Kaufmans, the Mandls and the Sylbers, decided to make Oswego their home.

Branko, now John, Kaufman; his wife, Kaethe (Kitty); and their daughter, Eva, went first to Washington, D.C., when the shelter closed. Eva recalled in an interview years later, a cousin of her mother who lived there "promised the world, but it wasn't forthcoming." The family then moved to Manhattan, where they lived for six months. They were not happy in New York City, however. Two Oswegonians who had befriended them while at the shelter, Dr. Golden Romney, a professor at the college, and Thomas Crabtree, the high school industrial arts teacher, happened to be in the city for a conference and visited the family while they were there. Romney and Crabtree urged Branko to return to Oswego and establish his photography business there.

The Kaufmans had good memories from their time at the shelter. In fact, recalled Eva, her father always talked about coming to the fort wearing old wooden clogs. He met a man from Oswego at the fence in the early days of the shelter, who asked Branko if the wooden clogs were what people wore where he came from. Branko replied no but said it was all he could find while fleeing Europe. The man asked Branko to wait by the fence, and a short time later, he returned with a pair of shoes. They were not quite the right size, but they were, he said, wonderful compared to what he had been wearing.

Eva also recalled the kindness of a nurse at the fort hospital who cared for her while she was isolated during the summer of 1945 with a case of scarlet fever. It was a difficult time, because Eva was young and all alone on the third floor of the hospital. Though her case was mild, she could interact only with hospital staff. Eva learned years later, the nurse who would visit her, read stories to her and play games with her was Oswego resident Jane Zaia.[320]

On September 16, 1946, the Kaufman Photography Studio opened at 21 West Bridge Street. The family liked Oswego so well, reported the *Palladium-Times*, that at the first opportunity, they decided to return. "The Kaufmans," the paper reported, "had taken out first citizenship papers and in five years expected to be citizens of the United States, and Oswegonians as well!"[321]

The Kaufmans were indeed good citizens and proud of their citizenship. In a letter to the *Palladium-Times* in October 1952 they urged their fellow Oswegonians to register and to vote. "We are two of your newest citizens." wrote John and Kitty Kaufman. "We who have experienced so much in lands where oppression reigns, prize and appreciate our citizenship because it means more to us than we can tell....[This] will be our first experience taking part in a free election in a free country and we hope you will all join with us on this happy occasion and perform your duty as citizens by registering and voting in the coming election."[322]

John Kaufman was active in Oswego's business and fraternal organizations, and his photographic skills were much sought after in the city. A profile in the December 1946 *Palladium-Times* described his work. "Wedding pictures, individual and group portraits and children's pictures are in the most demand and are quickly and economically accomplished at the Kaufman Photography Studio. Particular attention is given children's photography, often taking much more time and effort than seems profitable, but always producing individualistic results that continue to delight parents for years to come."[323]

Jane Zaia, the nurse who had cared for Eva at the fort hospital, in an interview years later, attested to John Kaufman's talents as a photographer, particularly in his work with children. He saw her with her young, red-haired little girl one day and asked Jane if he could have the privilege of taking the little girl's picture and Jane's as well. He refused any compensation for the photographs, she said. "I think it was a thank-you for being nice to his little girl. And believe me, it's the best picture I ever had!" Once John returned to Oswego and established his studio, Jane became one of his customers. "He was a marvelous photographer," she said. "He had an art that he picked out the best."[324] Jane's daughter Betsy Zaia Dorman recently remarked on the childhood pictures of herself and her sister, Cynthia, taken by John Kaufman, as being some of the best she's ever seen.[325]

Health considerations occasioned the Kaufman family's move to California in 1955. In a story in the *Palladium-Times*, John Kaufman expressed regret at having to leave Oswego and the people of the city who had been so good to them. Carl Stevens of Fulton purchased the Kaufman Photography Studio and said he intended to operate it under the Kaufman name.[326]

John Kaufman died on July 26, 1968, in Daly City, California, but was remembered by his friends in Oswego. His death was reported in the *Palladium-Times*.

John's daughter, Eva Kaufman Dye, graduated from Oswego High School and finished a year at Oswego State College before moving to California with her parents. She became a teacher, and looking back on her experiences at the shelter, she marveled at the teachers she and the other refugee students encountered. As a teacher herself, she said, "I don't know how they did it. With all those children from all over Europe, with all those different languages, but they did a wonderful job. Most of us went to college. We got our background in Oswego."

Eva continued to feel a special attachment to the city and came back for her fortieth high school reunion. "This is my home. My hometown. Even though I've been gone 40 years."[327]

Emmanuel Joseph Mandl and his wife, Maria Magdelena, remained in Oswego, residing at 21 East Bridge Street. Joseph operated a radio repair shop.

Jacob Fajnzylberg; his wife, Sarah; and their young son, Albert, who was born at the fort, found a home near the fort. Jake opened his own tailor shop, resuming a career he had started in Paris but was cut short by war.

The story of the Fort Ontario refugees and the Oswegonians comes full circle with those tailors who, separated by geography, religion, language, culture and experience, ultimately crossed paths in Oswego, New York.

A Tale of Three Tailors

In the spring of 1942, the war finally came to Joseph Spereno's door. He was among 1,346 men the Oswego Draft Board announced had registered for the draft and been given serial numbers, the step that would lead to the assignment of a permanent draft number.[328] At summer's end, he was called to active duty and was on his way to San Antonio, Texas, for training as a tail gunner for the U.S. Army Airs Corps.[329]

Jacob Fajnzylberg, in the meantime, continued to serve with the French Underground. His wife worked as a cook for sixty-eight Underground soldiers located in the French mountains near the Swiss border.[330] At some point, as concerns mounted about recapture by German soldiers, Fajnzylberg, his wife and son, Charles, began to make their way to Italy, ultimately joining a contingent of others displaced by the war.

The war was now in full force, and Joseph Spereno fully expected to be shipped far from home. Joe told his mother that he had chosen the U.S. Army Air Corps because he could not conceive of killing another person if he had to meet that person face to face. He knew training as a tail gunner would surely put him in harm's way, but he was determined to serve his country.[331] But Spereno was lucky. Well known for his singing and dancing talents as an Oswego High School student, he was rediscovered during his training. He had hosted a radio show and played with a jazz band, so Joe was quickly recruited by the Special Services Division of the air force. There, he played and sang with such entertainers as Jimmy Dorsey, Glenn Miller, the Andrews Sisters, Ella Fitzgerald and Lena Horne, to name a few.[332]

Tail gunner Joseph Spereno (*pictured bottom row, far right*) with his crew. *Ron Spereno photograph.*

While Joe Spereno served to boost the morale of war-weary soldiers, Jake Fajnzylberg and his family reached Italy, where the Allies were gaining ground and pushing back the Nazi advance. Fajnzylberg was lucky as well. Once he, his wife and son reached southern Italy, they heard of a unique opportunity. The United States, finally bowing to pressure from within its own borders and from its Allied partners, agreed to open a shelter within its borders for one thousand refugees from the Holocaust. Those selected would be moved to a place called Fort Ontario in Central New York State. The small city of twenty-two thousand sitting on one of the Great Lakes was called Oswego. It was Joe Spereno's hometown, and it would soon be home to the Fajnzylberg family as well.

Joe Spereno had spent his entire life in Oswego, New York. The harbor town on the south shore of Lake Ontario was a refuge for waves of immigrants from its founding in 1848 and continuing into the early years of the twentieth century.

Joe's father and mother came to Oswego from Italy. He lost his father when he was just five years old after he was killed in an accident involving an overturned vegetable truck. Joe was raised by his mother, Carolina, who did not speak English, but he was certainly able to communicate. Once, as a young child, while he was walking with his mother in the downtown area, Joe spied a suit in a store window that he insisted she buy for him. His mother said no, and Joe threw a fit. The confrontation with his mother over the suit attracted the attention of a local police officer, who feared young Joe was being abused by his mother. The fact that she spoke no English further complicated the situation.

Young Joseph Spereno, best dressed. *Oswego Music Hall of Fame, https://oswegomusichalloffame.com/inductee-bios-%26-photos.*

Once resolved, however, mother and son were sent on their way, and Joe ultimately got that suit. This incident may have been a precursor to Joe's early affinity for tailoring and smart dressing. By the time he was ready to graduate from Oswego High School, Joe was named "Best Dressed" in his class.[333] The 1941 yearbook, *The Paradox*, predicted that Joe would soon be working for a famous haberdasher on Fifth Avenue in New York City, where he would model all the latest men's fashions.[334]

Despite his temper tantrum over the shop window suit, Joe did learn the value of work from an early age. Joe's mother remarried after the death of Joe's father. Her second husband, Peter Fragale, owned a neighborhood restaurant. By the time he was fifteen, Joe had a job there as a bartender. Unlike most of his friends, Joe's work afforded him spending money, and he was generous with that extra cash. He often paid for his friends to go along to the movies with him.[335]

Jake Fajnzylberg and his wife, Sarah, along with their twelve-year-old son Charles, arrived at Fort Ontario on August 5, 1944. Once settled at the Fort, Fajnzylberg again took up the job of tailor, opening a shop to serve shelter residents. He continued to look after the tailoring needs of the shelter residents until the shelter closed.[336]

While in Oswego, he made the acquaintance of a local tailor named Jacob Kosoff, and in November 1944, he invited Kosoff to join him at his barracks home and then to see one of the shows put on at the shelter's Post Theater.

Oswego resident and attorney Samuel Tompkins, Kosoff's son-in-law, was invited as well as the guest of shelter resident Schnaynam Salby. Mae Kosoff Tompkins and her husband were already familiar with and supportive of the refugees. It was Mae who had provided the ring for the wedding of shelter residents Manya Hart-Myer to Ernest Bruer a few months earlier.

The presence of Kosoff and Tompkins caused a bit of confusion, however, because at that point, outsiders were not entitled to attend the shows at the Post Theater. The shelter's acting security chief, J.L. Carroll, related in his report about the incident that the invitation was not meant to break the shelter rules.[337]

The friendships between these refugees and these Oswegonians continued nonetheless, and when Fajnzylberg decided to return to Oswego after living for a short time in Chicago, he purchased Kosoff's tailoring business.

Jacob Kosoff passed away in March 1947. Soon after, Jacob Fajnzylberg, who had, by then, changed his name to Jake Sylber, took over the Kosoff Tailor Shop.[338] Jake Sylber was a fixture in the Oswego business community for nearly a decade, operating his shop at 3 West Bridge Street.

Joe Spereno, home from the war, walked into Sylber's tailor shop one day, expressed interest in learning the trade and asked to be Sylber's apprentice. Despite his musical talent, Joe said the entertainment industry was no place for a family man, so he gave that up to become a tailor instead.[339]

Jane Zaia worked as a nurse at the Oswego Hospital, assisted at the shelter hospital and continued her nursing career once the shelter closed. She recalled organizing a party to celebrate her daughter's fourth birthday and asked her to make a list of friends to invite. Cynthia listed some of her playmates in the neighborhood and then said, "And don't forget my new friend 'Fort Ontario Albert.'" "Who is 'Fort Ontario Albert?'" Jane asked, and Jane's mother said he was from one of the refugee families who now lived up the street. Jane delivered the invitation to Fort Ontario Albert's

"Fort Ontario Albert" is pictured at a birthday party for Cynthia Zaia (Beraud). The arrow points to Albert. Cynthia is just in front of Albert, third from left. *Special Collections, Penfield Library, State University of New York at Oswego.*

mother, Sarah Sylber. Albert arrived at the party with a present for Cynthia, but when it was time to leave, Jane told her daughter to thank each of her guests for bringing a gift. When she thanked Albert, he promptly took back his gift until his mother explained to him that birthday gifts were meant to be left for the birthday girl. They remained friends and playmates until both families moved, and Jane remembered that Jake Sylber and his family were very well thought of around town.[340]

The Sylber family relocated to California in the mid-1950s, but before they left, Jake Sylber thanked his adopted home community for the support extended to him from the time he entered the fort on August 5, 1944, in a letter to the *Palladium-Times*.

> *We have spent our happiest years here. We came here unknown, without friends and without means of a livelihood. The people of Oswego immediately accepted us. They made us feel that we once again belonged to a community, that we once again had friends.*
>
> *When I opened my tailor shop, the businessmen invited me into their organizations. They said, "Jake, you are one of us."*
>
> *My oldest son, Charles, was educated in the Oswego schools. He entered the Army from Oswego and happily served his country. It is something my wife and I are very proud of.*
>
> *My youngest son, Albert, was born at the Fort and he has attended local schools. He wants me to let everyone know that he will miss all of his friends.*
>
> *It is not easy to leave such a marvelous community and wonderful friends. We want to thank everyone for what they have done for us and for their good wishes for our future.*[341]

Jake Sylber was able to leave the tailor shop in good hands. His young apprentice, Joseph Spereno, took over the shop and operated it for the next twenty-two years.

On June 16, 1945, Joe married Mary Margaret Raby. Together, they raised four children.

Joe's youngest son, Ron, remembers the tailor shop well. It shared space with the WOSC radio station, just off the west side of the bridge. "When he took over the tailor shop, my father always served the firemen and policemen for free, sewing their badges and their uniforms for them. Oswego policemen all had a key to his shop so they could come in and get warm from the bad weather and the big window in the shop allowed them to continue to observe their beat."

Spereno's Tailor Shop at 3 West Bridge Street shared the building with the WOSC radio station. The tailor shop sign is visible in the window on the left. *Oswego County Historical Society.*

Ron spent a lot of time in the tailor shop as a kid, and he recalled the big, old equipment there. Both his parents worked, so Ron was there often on weekends and when he was not in school. "A lot of the older Italian men in the city liked to congregate there and share stories," said Ron. "It was more like a barbershop! But then my dad would tell them he had to get back to work." Joe did all the tailoring for the city's men's shops at that time.

Ron said his father was "the smartest man I ever knew, well read and with an answer for all my questions." He had a big, booming voice that Ron said could sometimes intimidate his friends, but he wasn't yelling at any of them. His voice was just naturally loud.

Like most Italian men of his generation, Joe was stern and strict, especially, Ron remembered, with his sister, because Italian women were particularly protected. No matter what, he wanted the best for his children and more than what he had. "To get a compliment from him," said Ron, "was as if God himself came down and gave you the compliment."

And he raised his children "without prejudices. We were not allowed to call anyone by a prejudicial slang term…or to steal. He said even if you use a pen in a bank, that pen is not yours. It belongs to the bank, so don't take it."

Ron recalled that his father loved fishing and would go out twice a week. While he never resumed singing professionally, Ron recalled his father did sing at his sister's wedding.

153

After more than two decades at 3 West Bridge Street, Joe Spereno had to close the tailor shop when the WOSC radio station wanted to expand. Joe was in his late fifties then, but, always the worker, he took a job in the laundry department at the Fitzpatrick nuclear facility just outside Oswego. In 1990, he was given the key to the city of Oswego in recognition of his musical accomplishments during World War II.[342]

At the urging of his son Charles, who had spent time on the West Coast while in the service, Jake Sylber relocated with his wife, Sarah, and their young son Albert to California. The big city of Los Angeles was not to Jake's liking, however, so he explored the area and settled on Oxnard, a coastal town outside of Los Angeles. There, he set up a tailoring business at 447 Oxnard Boulevard.[343]

Jake Sylber had come a very long way from the beaches of Dunkirk and from Oswego, New York, but he had found a home at last. Jake and Sarah Sylber lived in California until their deaths.

Charles Sylber graduated from Oswego High School in January 1951 and joined the United States Army. He had occasion to visit the Safe Haven Holocaust Refugee Shelter Museum after it was established. There, he saw a picture of himself as a young man standing near the fort fence. Charles Sylber passed away in 2017 at the age of eighty-seven.[344]

Albert Sylber, "Fort Ontario Albert," joined the service as well. He trained in Florida to be a naval flight officer.[345] He was a physician and a Bronze Star medalist in the Vietnam War, a Vietnam army and navy veteran and an emergency room physician at HCA Greenview Hospital in Bowling Green, Kentucky. Albert passed away in Bowling Green on December 13, 1990, at the age of forty-five.[346]

Epilogue

The Republican and the Liberal

Richard "Rosie" Rosenbaum spent his formative years in Oswego. His maternal grandparents, Max and Bessie Gover, ran Gover's Department Store on the outskirts of the city near "the forks of the road" at 173 West Seneca Street. Richard and his parents lived in the apartment above the store. Theirs was one of about ten Jewish families then living in the city. Growing up in the 1930s, he was aware of the rise of anti-Semitism and experienced it himself at the hands of other kids in town.

In his autobiography, Rosenbaum recalled an incident that prompted shouting on the part of his normally mild-mannered father, Jack Rosenbaum. A person came to their door raising money for Father Charles Coughlin, the Catholic priest and radio personality who espoused isolationist and anti-Semitic views. His father told the solicitor to get off his porch and that he should be ashamed of himself.

As a schoolboy, Rosenbaum encountered heckling and name-calling. His hair had begun to fall out by the time he was eight, a result of alopecia, a condition in which hair follicles starve due to a minor circulatory malfunction. At the time, not much was known about the condition. Despite medical consultations and remedies, his hair continued to fall out. "I grew up hearing the taunts of grammar school kids making fun of me," he remembered, "and by the time I was a teenager I was pretty sensitive. At an age when appearance often seems all-important, I looked pretty strange." Rosenbaum was also the only Jewish child in his elementary school, and that is where, he says, "I first experienced [anti-Semitism's] bitter taste.

Richard Rosenbaum as a Star Scout in Oswego, age thirteen, August 1944. *From* No Room for Democracy: The Triumph of Ego over Common Sense, *Richard Rosenbaum (Rochester, NY, RIT Press, 2008).*

"As I grew older, the taunts grew worse. Often as I walked to and from school, I had to endure name-calling—'Kike!' 'Dirty Jew'—and sometimes I'd be attacked by kids who would jump me." He recalled one kid in particular who was a constant irritant, but by the time Rosenbaum reached the seventh grade, he was bigger and stronger. He said, "I finally corked the kid on the nose; he never came near me again."

Living on a Great Lake had its advantages, and these softened the sting of prejudice, bringing plenty of happy times in his early years as well. Lake Ontario's beaches provided summer fun with his friends. The Oswego River teemed with fish, and early mornings would find him on the river's banks, hauling in stringers full of bass, perch and pike. He also joined Boy Scout Troop 5, where he became patrol leader and the highest-ranking member of the troop.

His six-foot-two-inch height by the time he was thirteen made Rosenbaum the star of the local basketball team. He was always the highest scorer but never made captain, saying it would have been unthinkable at that time in Upstate New York to have a Jewish kid named team captain.

Rosenbaum's size presented another advantage. A boarder at the Rosenbaum home, who was a freshman at the college, told him about summer job openings at the fort. It was to open as an emergency shelter for Holocaust refugees, and local people were being hired for a variety of jobs. Even though he was fourteen, Rosenbaum lied about his age, saying he was sixteen. He soon found himself part of the grounds crew at the fort, preparing for the arrival of the refugees. "I will never forget my first sight of those families, carrying their cardboard suitcases, exhausted, confused, frightened, half-starved, their eyes haunted by past terrors," he recalled.[347]

Mane and Jelka Hochwald and their young son, Branko, were among the 982 refugees who arrived at the fort that day. They had escaped the Nazis, leaving Yugoslavia, making their way through the Balkans, and finally arriving in Italy in 1941. By 1944, Mane, Jelka and nine-year-old Branko were in a detainee camp in Calabria, but with the intervention of the American president and a good bit of luck, the family was selected to board the *Henry Gibbins* and head to shelter in the United States.

Branko enjoyed his new life in America, although his first days at School No. 2 were challenging. He sat in the classroom with his good friend from the shelter Ivo Hirschler. They had acquired some knowledge of the English language in the first few weeks at the fort, but it did not help as his teacher began the morning lesson.[348]

Despite a challenging beginning with the English language, Branko acclimated well to shelter life. He joined the Cub Scout troop, worked hard to learn English and found that the town's children were very friendly. He said he experienced no anti-Semitism. It was, he said in an interview years later, "an idyllic existence for children."[349]

Once the shelter closed, the Hochwald family relocated to the New York City area. Mane, who had been a wood merchant in Yugoslavia and who served as a labor leader at the fort shelter, began work as a waiter, summers in the Catskills and winters at the Commodore Hotel. Jelka became a chef. She also made candy on an assembly line. Branko changed his name to Raymond B. Harding. He took the name Harding from the title character of his favorite radio program, *David Harding, Counterspy*. His parents changed their last name to Harding as well. Ray worked his way through school, waiting tables and driving a cab. He graduated from New York University's School of Law.[350]

Richard Rosenbaum completed his summer job at the Fort but not before his mother convinced him to drop off his comic book collection for the young children at the shelter. "As a young boy I owned a large supply of comic books," he recalled in a letter to the Safe Haven Museum. "In those days *Captain Marvel*, *Superman* and all that kind of thing were popular. My mother, who is a charitable type, asked me if I would give the comic books to the children in the Fort, which I readily agreed to do." His mother drove him over to the fort, the back seat of the car filled with comic books. No sooner did he get out of the car in the parking lot than he was surrounded by circles of children. "I handed them all comic books. They were very excited and very happy to get these comic books."[351]

The Rosenbaum family relocated to Rochester, New York, when Richard was fourteen. There, nearly all the kids in his neighborhood were Jewish. Still, he was initially reluctant to leave Oswego. "In thinking back over my years in Oswego," he reflected in his autobiography, "I realize I did have some good friends and many good times….As I came to understand my confrontational personality, I learned to make an extra effort to get along with people. That habit, I'm sure, stood me in good stead later in the world of politics and government."[352]

Oswego native Richard Rosenbaum and Fort Ontario Emergency Refugee Shelter resident Branko Hochwald, now Ray Harding, entered the world of New York politics and rose to great heights. Whether by natural inclination or through their experience with discrimination in their early years, both were certainly suited to that rough-and-tumble world.

Richard Rosenbaum graduated from Hobart College in Upstate New York and went on to law school at Cornell University. He entered local politics as Republican chair of the town of Penfield, but in six short years, he rose to become the GOP chair of Monroe County.[353] He was among the youngest to be elected state supreme court justice but later left the bench when former governor Nelson Rockefeller asked him to chair the State Republican Party. He made a brief run for governor in 1982 and a second run in 1994, when he lost to former governor George Pataki.[354]

Ray Harding took the liberal route in New York politics. Alex Rose, a garment workers union leader, launched the Liberal Party in 1944, the same year Ray Harding came to the Fort Ontario Emergency Refugee Shelter. When Rose died in 1976, Harding took over the party.[355] He enjoyed a long career as a political rainmaker.

> *While the Liberal Party always remained relatively small, Harding, a big, chain-smoking figure some said perfectly fit the caricature of a political boss, made the most of it.*
>
> *He helped Mario Cuomo get elected governor and…worked to catapult Rudy Giuliani into the mayor's office.…However, his last years* [in politics] *were darkened by his ties to a pay-to-play pension fund scheme tied to former State Comptroller Alan Hevesi.*[356]

Raymond Harding spoke at the 1981 reunion and dedication of a memorial plaque at Fort Ontario.[357] At the time, he was chair of the New York Liberal Party and a special assistant to then governor Hugh Carey. Harding said on that day:

> *I believe we were brought here not without reason or purpose. We bear a special responsibility. No generation of Americans, no segment of American society has a greater duty, has a greater obligation than we, the Oswego Refugees…to make certain that no American is denied a decent place in this society, that no American is treated in this homeland as second-class citizen, as a refugee.*[358]

Republican Richard Rosenbaum and Liberal Ray Harding were often called upon to represent their respective parties in political debates. Decades after both had left Oswego, the two politicos met in New York City for a debate. They began talking with each other about where they were from and discovered their Oswego connection. Harding told Rosenbaum he was a young kid at the shelter and didn't recall much about his experiences there, except for one thing. He remembered an older boy from Oswego who came to the shelter with lots of comic books and that he was part of a circle of kids who surrounded the kid from Oswego giving out comic books. Richard Rosenbaum smiled at Ray Harding and said, "I was that kid."[359]

An Encore for an Operetta Lost, Then Found

Charles Abeles, the composer of the operetta *The Golden Cage*, opted to return to his native Austria once the shelter closed. On his way, he stopped in New York City to contact a publisher to print the music he had written while living at the fort, including several songs, three operettas and piano music. Tragically, that publisher stole all his music.

Charles's nephew Peter Koppitz recalled:

> *His wife had survived the war in Mödling and he returned to her and to Austria in 1946, but like most returnees, he felt the same way—society didn't want to have anything to do with the emigrants. His previous contacts were absent, and no one was interested in his compositions. He wrote another operetta,* The Dollar Princess, *but wherever he submitted it, it came back. Many of his compositions have been lost; he had given them to others who would not give them back. And so he wrote nothing more because he was convinced that what was in his head nobody could steal from him. With a small pension, with music lessons and the supervision of children, he earned his living. Only relatives and friends were able to enjoy his music. On April 17, 1987 he died in Brunn am Gebirge.*[360]

"Many discoveries result from coincidences, accidental contacts, and just plain luck," said Marilynn Smiley, musicologist and retired professor of music at the State University of New York at Oswego.

> *Even though I had lived in Oswego for several years, I had not been aware of the Fort Ontario Emergency Refugee Shelter until my neighbor, Ralph*

Faust, showed me phonograph records containing original chamber music compositions by Leon Levitch, a former refugee at the shelter, who had studied at the high school. This prompted me to read Ruth Gruber's book, which mentions many musical activities by the refugees, and to realize that a study of their musical events warranted further research.

Aware of Smiley's interest in the musical activities of the shelter residents, the curator of the Safe Haven Museum called Smiley to connect her with visitors who had come to the museum.

Peter Koppitz of Germany had come to the United States to visit friends. He recalled his uncle had said his most pleasant years were spent in Oswego, so Peter decided to visit the city for himself. Peter met with Smiley, and she relayed her research interest in the shelter's music.

Upon his return to Germany, Peter discovered a forgotten trunk in his brother's home that contained possessions of his uncle Charles Abeles. In it was a rough draft of *The Golden Cage*. He mailed the incomplete copy to Marilynn Smiley, who was then serving as president of the board of directors of the Oswego Opera Theater. "Imagine my surprise to receive a thick manilla envelope from Mr. Koppitz containing a musical score. It was a draft of *The Golden Cage*…[but] many of the songs had no text and no accompaniment," said Smiley. "I started searching for the text, and after mentioning my quest to Paul Lear, Site Manager of Fort Ontario, in a casual conversation, I learned that he had the text right here in Oswego!"

Lear had discovered the libretto to the operetta in the National Archives.

In 2020, Juan LaManna, the artistic director of Oswego Opera Theater, edited and completed the score, put the words to music and orchestrated it. Nearly seventy-seven years after its first and only performance, *The Golden Cage* took to the stage once again at the Waterman Theater at SUNY Oswego on November 12 and 13, 2022. LaManna and Benjamin Spierman, a faculty member at Rutgers University with connections to the Bronx Opera Company, codirected the production, which featured cast members from New York City, Central New York and Oswego.

Smiley noted that the original intent of the operetta was to convince immigration and other federal government employees that the fort refugees should be allowed to remain in the United States. The issues the fort refugees faced then—immigration quotas, anti-Semitism, war and diversity—are still prominent issues today, making *The Golden Cage* as relevant now as it was in 1945.[361]

CONCLUSION

Years after the Fort Ontario Emergency Refugee Shelter closed, Walter Greenberg, who was a young boy when he arrived there, reflected on the dichotomy of his experiences during the war.

I have a poem that I think says it better than anything I could say, and I think it was…part of the collection I Will Never See Another Butterfly *from Terezin, and this little girl talks about leaving their home and subsequently what her reflections are on it.…The poem, really for me, explains well how I felt then, even how I feel now, and how…this relationship was established between us and the Oswego children, because I think it worked both ways; it was a two-way street. We wanted to be like them, and they saw something in us.*

Bird Song

He doesn't know the world at all
Who stays in his nest and doesn't go out.
He doesn't know what birds know best,
Nor what I want to sing about, that the world is full of loneliness.
When dewdrops sparkle in the grass,
and there is a flood with morning light,
a blackbird sings upon a bush,
to greet the dawning after night.

Then, I know how fine it is to live.
Hey, try to open your heart to beauty,
Go to the woods someday and weave a wreath of memory there.
Then if the tears obscure your way,
You will know how wonderful it is to be alive.

I think that we projected this feeling to the Oswegonians, of how wonderful it is to be alive, and I think they reciprocated in being kind to us.

Greenberg also reflected on the importance of preserving and retelling the story of the Fort Ontario Emergency Refugee Shelter. "I think it's important to study what happened, not because of us 982 refugees, but more important, historically, what happened to a country and more specifically to a world which I [believe engaged in] 'world amnesia.' I think so much was overlooked conveniently by good people. The bad guys are easy to identify. The question is, what could the good guys have done to make it a little bit easier…for more people to survive?"[362]

Walter Greenberg (*holding drill*) and his classmates work on a boat-building project at Campus School on the Oswego Teachers College campus. (The boat sank in the lake on its inaugural launch.) *Special Collections, Penfield Library, State University of New York at Oswego.*

ERNEST BRAUN, THE CHEMIST who perfected a groundbreaking treatment for presurgical wound care while at Fort Ontario, reflected on his experience in Oswego in a letter to Judge George Penney after Braun served as a guest speaker at a meeting of the Oswego Rotary Club in the summer of 1945. In the letter's conclusion, he said it was his firm conviction that "if every man would clasp hands with his fellow man, if all human beings would help each other to survive, Humanity would have a MIGHTY WHEEL of SERVICE and UNDERSTANDING which is the basis of all religion— [the] foundation of all ethics."[363]

"To study the Holocaust is to descend into a world devoid of humanity," says *Dr. Lawrence Baron in the introduction to* Haven from the Holocaust: Oswego, New York, 1944–46. *For the 982 refugees from the Holocaust, the people of Oswego supplied that lost humanity. Beyond bicycles, dolls, ping-pong balls and even education, this humanity was probably the greatest gift any individual or any community could possibly have offered.*

Notes

Preface

1. Gruber, *Haven*, 230.

Introduction

2. "Surprised by Friends on Her 16th Birthday," *Oswego Palladium-Times*, April 8, 1940, 2.
3. "Local Man Escaped Nazi Gas Chambers," *Press-Courier* (Oxnard, CA), October 13, 1955, 3.
4. "Author Aims for Wide Audience, Targets Fort Ontario," *Oswego Palladium-Times*, June 10, 1999.

Chapter 1

5. Paul Lear, "The War Refugee Board and the Origins of the Fort Ontario Emergency Refugee Shelter," Historic Fort Ontario, https://historicfortontario.com/see-history-alive/.
6. Lawrence Baron, Michael Dobkowsky interview, oral history 218 MS 131, Special Collections, Penfield Library, SUNY Oswego.

7. David Wyman oral interview, Fort Ontario Refugee Project, Special Collections, Penfield Library, SUNY Oswego, September 23, 1986.
8. *Encyclopedia of America's Response to the Holocaust*, "Grafton, Samuel," http://enc.wymaninstitute.org/?p=219.
9. Samuel Grafton oral interview, Special Collections, Penfield Library, SUNY Oswego, tape 269, 1983–86.
10. Ibid.
11. National Archives, "'Acquiescence' Memo, January 13, 1944," https://www.docsteach.org/documents/document/acquiescence-memo.
12. Samuel Grafton oral interview, 1983–86.
13. Lear, "War Refugee Board."
14. Samuel Grafton oral interview, 1983–86.
15. Marks, Krug and Myer, *Token Shipment*, 15.
16. Ibid., 16.
17. Jim Cheney, "Uncovering American History at Fort Ontario in Oswego, New York," Uncovering New York, October 24, 2022, https://uncoveringnewyork.com/fort-ontario-oswego/.
18. Paul Lear, "History of the Fort," Historic Fort Ontario, https://historicfortontario.com/see-history-alive/.
19. Paul Lear, superintendent of Fort Ontario State Historic Site, presenter, "Fort Ontario Is My Camp," presentation at the Fort Ontario Conference on History and Archaeology, March 25, 2023.

Chapter 2

20. Jack Gould, "Oswego Acts Host to United Nations," *New York Times*, June 14, 1943, 19.
21. "United Nations Broadcast Heard by Whole Nation," *Oswego Palladium-Times*, June 14, 1943, 12.
22. Dr. Seward Salisbury oral interview, Special Collections, Penfield Library, SUNY at Oswego, tape 274, November 1983.
23. Fort Ontario, "Fort Ontario Celebrates Black History Month," Facebook, February 8, 2023.
24. Paul Lear, "Buffalo Soldiers and Fort Ontario: Oswego, NY, 1908–1911," Historic Fort Ontario, https://historicfortontario.com/see-history-alive/.
25. "What People Say," *Oswego Palladium-Times*, August 24, 1944, 7.
26. Marks, Krug and Myer, *Token Shipment*, 18.
27. William Joyce Sr. interview, May 17, 2023.

28. Mark List, "Reflections on Pearl Harbor and World War II," *Island Sand Paper*, September 18, 2001, 18. SH-5, Harold Clark Collection, Special Collections, Penfield Library, SUNY Oswego.

29. Eisenhower Foundation, "War Service Medal," https://www.eisenhowerfoundation.net/primary-source/item/war-service-medal.

30. Ibid.

31. Rogers, *Oswego*, 177.

32. Ibid., 193.

33. "War Department to Put Fort on Standby Basis," *Oswego Palladium-Times*, February 10, 1944, 4.

34. "War Refugees to Come from Spain, France, Balkans," *Oswego Palladium-Times*, June 10, 1944, 2.

35. "Says Oswego May Emulate Example Set by Scranton," *Oswego Palladium-Times*, March 28, 1944, 18.

36. "1000 War Refugees Coming to Oswego," *Oswego Palladium-Times*, June 9, 1944, 1, 4.

37. William Joyce Sr. interview; Mary Helen Crisafulli Colloca interview, May 18, 2023.

38. Mary Helen Crisafulli Colloca interview, May 18, 2023.

39. "War Refugees to Come," *Oswego Palladium-Times*, 2.

40. Ibid., 6.

41. "Discusses Fort Refugee Center," *Oswego Palladium-Times*, June 16, 1944, 5.

42. "President Glad That Refuge Plan Pleases Oswego," *Oswego Palladium-Times*, June 24, 1944, 4.

43. "Japs Discuss Refugee Camp," *Oswego Palladium-Times*, June 27, 1944, 4.

44. "Work Starts to Make Fort into Refugee Center," *Oswego Palladium-Times*, July 7, 1944, 7.

45. "Select Director of Refugee Camp," *Oswego Palladium-Times*, July 8, 1944, 4.

46. "War Relocation Authority Head at Fort Ontario," *Oswego Palladium-Times*, July 11, 1944, 4.

47. "Asserts Refugee Camp Operations to Benefit City," *Oswego Palladium-Times*, July 12, 1944, 1, 4.

48. "To Collect Toys for Children at Refugee Center," *Oswego Palladium-Times*, July 14, 1944, 4.

49. "Gathering Staff to Handle Work at Fort Ontario," *Oswego Palladium-Times*, July 15, 1944, 4.

50. "General Terry Here to See Refugee Center at Fort," *Oswego Palladium-Times*, July 20, 1944, 4.

51. "Will Turn Fort Over This Week to WRA Director," *Oswego Palladium-Times*, July 24, 1944, 4.
52. Florence Mahaney Farley interview, July 19, 2023.
53. "30 Barracks at Fort Ready for 1,000 Refugees," *Oswego Palladium-Times*, July 26, 1944, 4.
54. "No Saboteurs or Spies Coming to Refugees Center," *Oswego Palladium-Times*, July 27, 1944, 2.
55. "War Refugees to Arrive at Fort Saturday," *Oswego Palladium-Times*, August 4, 1944, 4.
56. "984 European War Refugees Reach Fort," *Oswego Palladium-Times*, August 5, 1944, 12.

Chapter 3

57. Mary Helen Crisafulli Colloca interview, May 2023
58. Frances Ruggio Enwright interview, February 2023.
59. "Eva Rosenfeld Passes," *New Ontario Chronicle*, January 2020, 6.
60. Gruber, *Haven*, 105–8.
61. United States Holocaust Memorial Museum, "Adam Munz Oral Interview," 1991, https://collections.ushmm.org/search/catalog/irn512579.
62. Ibid.
63. Ibid.
64. "Refugee Ping Pong," letter from Lawrence Carroll to Scott Scanlon, Safe Haven Museum, May 29, 2000, Special Collections, Penfield Library, SUNY Oswego, SH 11 02.1.4.
65. Safe Haven: Oswego Reunion, oral history 271, August 1984, Special Collections, Penfield Library, SUNY Oswego.
66. Lowenstein, *Token Refuge*, 163.
67. Elaine Gagas Cost interview, March 28, 2023.
68. Adam Munz obituary, *Newsday*, January 15, 1988, 50.
69. Legacy.com, "Lawrence Carroll Obituary, Published in the *Auburn Citizen*, November 11, 2014," https://www.legacy.com/us/obituaries/auburnpub/name/lawrence-carroll-obituary?id=10570546.
70. Lowenstein, *Token Refuge*, 180.
71. Frances Enwright interview, February 2023.
72. Ibid.
73. Warnes, Hill, Fisher, Kahl, Coe-Rappaport, *Don't Fence Me In*, 1.
74. Frances Enwright interview.

Chapter 4

75. Safe Haven: Jack Bass interview for a WSLU North Country Public Radio documentary, 1983, Oswego Public Library, Digital Collection, http://www.nyheritage.org/about/#copyright.

76. Safe Haven: Oral history interview with Jack Bass, oral history 270, Special Collections, Penfield Library, SUNY Oswego.

77. Warnes, Hill, Fisher, Kahl, Coe-Rappaport, *Don't Fence Me In*, 91.

78. Sylvain Boni letter, Special Collections, Penfield Library, SUNY Oswego, SH 11, 02.5 Boni.

79. Ibid., 93.

80. Rolf Manfred Kuznitzki, letter to Liz Kahl, March 26, 2001, Safe Haven Museum, SH 11 Special Collections, Penfield Library, SUNY Oswego.

81. Ibid.

82. Safe Haven: Oral history interview with Geraldine Desens Rossiter, oral history 279, Special Collections, Penfield Library, SUNY Oswego.

83. Ibid.

84. Gruber, *Haven*, 155–56.

85. Rossiter interview.

86. Ibid.

87. Ibid.

88. Gruber, *Haven*, 295.

89. "Reception Moves Refugees Deeply at Fort Ontario," *Oswego Palladium-Times*, August 7, 1944, 4.

90. "Oswego Merchants Will Supply Needs of War Refugees," *Oswego Palladium-Times*, August 8, 1944, 12.

91. Letter from Linda Shapiro Weinstein to Judy Coe Rapaport, President Safe Haven Museum board, August 22, 2003, Safe Museum Collection.

92. "Stories From Oswego's Cemeteries," in *Don't Fence Me In*, 29.

93. Ibid.

94. "Seek Barbering, Other Services for Fort Group," *Oswego Palladium-Times*, August 11, 1944, 7.

95. Baron, *Haven from the Holocaust*, 18.

96. Letter from Mr. and Mrs. James Scandura to Safe Haven Museum, March 12, 2001.

97. "Oswego Friendly to War Refugees," *Oswego Palladium-Times*, August 15, 1944, 12.

98. "Children Hold Fitzhugh Park Athletic Meet," *Oswego Palladium-Times*, August 26, 1944, 5.

99. "Refugee Couple Wed at Shelter," *Oswego Palladium-Times*, August 17, 1944, 4.

100. "Holocaust Refugees Gaze Fondly on Oswego," *Oswego Palladium-Times*, April 11, 1990, 4.

101. "Second Refugee Couple Married," *Oswego Palladium-Times*, August 21, 1944, 4.

102. "Local Advisory Group for Fort Shelter Chosen," *Oswego Palladium-Times*, August 22, 1944, 4.

103. Letter from Joel Lasky to Safe Haven Museum.

104. "Favors Refugee Children Going to School Here," *Oswego Palladium-Times*, August 25, 1944, 12.

Chapter 5

105. Wikipedia, "Ruth Gruber," https://en.wikipedia.org/wiki/Ruth_Gruber.

106. Emily Langer, "Ruth Gruber, Who Accompanied 1,000 Jews to the Shores of the United States During the Holocaust, Dies at 105," *Washington Post*, November 19, 2016, https://www.washingtonpost.com/national/ruth-gruber-who-accompanied-1000-jews-to-the-shores-of-the-united-states-during-the-holocaust-dies-at-105/2016/11/17/da16277c-ad12-11e6-8b45-f8e493f06fcd_story.html.

107. Ibid.

108. Gruber, *Haven*, 180–82.

109. Justin White, Oswego County historian, letter to Paul Lear and Judy Coe Rapaport, July 5, 2019, Fort Ontario archives.

110. Gruber, *Haven*, 180–82.

111. "Edwin Morey Waterbury Dies; *Palladium-Times* Publisher, Civic Leader," *Oswego Palladium-Times*, December 31, 1952, 3.

112. Charles "Chip" Tobey interview, April 11, 2023.

113. "Waterbury Dies," *Oswego Palladium-Times*, 3.

114. "Facts Stated by Committee About Refugee Shelter," *Oswego Palladium-Times*, August 29, 1944, 5.

115. "Permanent Organization of the Oswego Citizens Fort Ontario Permanent Advisory Committee," Safe Haven Museum.

116. "Facts Stated by Committee," *Oswego Palladium-Times*, 5.

117. "Hundreds Coming During Week-End to See Refugees," *Oswego Palladium-Times*, August 28, 1944, 16.

118. "Hundreds Arrive for Week-End at Refugee Shelter," *Oswego Palladium-Times*, September 1, 1944, 15.

119. "Thousands Will Visit Shelter at Fort on Sunday," *Oswego Palladium-Times*, September 2, 1944, 12.

120. Gruber, *Haven*, 192–93.

121. "More Than 10,000 Made Inspection of Fort Shelter," *Oswego Palladium-Times*, September 5, 1944, 12.

122. Baron, *Haven from the Holocaust*, 14.

123. "Fiction, Fact About Refugees," *Oswego Palladium-Times*, September 5, 1944, 4.

124. "What People Say," *Oswego Palladium-Times*, October 31, 1944, 8.

125. Lowenstein, *Token Refuge*, 73–74.

126. Ibid.

127. Eleanor Roosevelt, "My Day," *Kansas City* (MO) *Star*, September 24, 1944, Oswego County Historical Society scrapbook.

Chapter 6

128. Joseph Smart oral history interview, July 10, 1984, oral history 273, Special Collections, Penfield Library, SUNY at Oswego.

129. Smith, "Influence of Ralph M. Faust," 29.

130. "Refugee Writes About Shopping Trip into City," *Oswego Palladium-Times*, August 31, 1944, 5.

131. "Edmund Landau: I Walk in the City," in *Don't Fence Me In*, 51.

132. "C.C. Gagas, Restauranteur Dies at 76," *Post Standard*, March 13, 1971, 6.

133. "Our Business Leaders in the Public Eye," *Oswego Palladium-Times*, June 20, 1948, 10.

134. Chris Gagas interview, March 21, 2023.

135. Cost, *Essays*, 45.

136. Elaine Gagas Cost interview.

137. "1st Refugees Will Leave Fort by February 6," *Oswego Palladium-Times*, January 19, 1946, 10.

138. Lowenstein, *Token Refuge*, 174.

139. Naomi Jolles, "Oswego Refugees Only Want a Chance to Learn," *New York Post*, August 8, 1944, 5.

Chapter 7

140. Marks, Krug and Myer, *Token Shipment*, 48.

141. Warnes, Hill, Fisher, Kahl, Coe-Rappaport, *Don't Fence Me In*, 59.

142. "Investigation of Problems Presented by Refugees at Fort Ontario Refugee Shelter," 49.

143. Ibid., 57.

144. Virginia Dean oral interview, November 29, 1983, oral history 278, Special Collections, Penfield Library, SUNY Oswego.

145. Ibid.

146. Ibid., 59.

147. Ibid.

148. "Investigation of Problems Presented by Refugees at Fort Ontario Refugee Shelter," 67.

149. Joseph Langnas interview transcript, August 12, 1998, United States Holocaust Memorial Museum.

150. Ruth Gruber oral interview, oral history 270, Special Collections, Penfield Library, SUNY Oswego.

151. Gruber, *Haven*, 258.

152. Ibid., 178.

153. Letter from Sylvain Boni, Special Collections, Penfield Library, SUNY Oswego, SH 5, 02.5.

154. "Investigation of Problems Presented by Refugees at Fort Ontario Refugee Shelter," 69.

155. Ibid., 69.

156. Ibid., 71.

157. Warnes, Hill, Fisher, Kahl, Coe-Rappaport, *Don't Fence Me In*, 31.

158. Ibid.

159. Ibid.

160. Walter Greenberg oral interview, January 26, 1984, oral history 275, Special Collections, Penfield Library, SUNY Oswego.

161. "Investigation of Problems Presented by Refugees at Fort Ontario Refugee Shelter," 60.

162. Naomi Jolles, "The Fourth R," *Women's Home Companion*, July 1945, 16, 32.

Chapter 8

163. Ibid., 16, 32.

164. Smith, "Influence of Ralph M. Faust," 21–23.

165. Ralph Faust interview transcript, June 29, 1986, Oswego County Historical Society, Safe Haven Collection, 8.

166. Ralph Faust oral interview, November 19, 1983, oral history 278, Special Collections, Penfield Library, SUNY Oswego.

167. Steffi Steinberg Winters oral interview, January 26, 1984, oral history 280, Special Collections, Penfield Library, SUNY Oswego.

168. Faust interview.

169. "162 Children at Refugee Shelter Going to School," *Oswego Palladium-Times*, August 29, 1944, 5.

170. Ibid.

171. Margaret Greene Crisafulli interview, May 9, 2023.

172. Smith, "Influence of Ralph M. Faust," 27.

173. Gruber, *Haven*, 181–82.

174. Jolles, "Fourth R," 16, 32.

175. Ibid.

176. Rolf Manfred Kuznitzki, letter to Elizabeth Kahl, Special Collections, Penfield Library, SUNY Oswego.

177. Michelle Reed, "When Oswego Was a Haven," *Oswego Alumni* 29, no. 1 (Spring 2003): 15.

178. Rolf Manfred Kuznitzki, letter to Elizabeth Kahl, Special Collections, Penfield Library, SUNY Oswego, SH 11.

179. "Legion Speaking Contest Tuesday," *Oswego Palladium-Times*, December 10, 1944, 2.

180. Liz Harris, "Berkeley Architect Reconstructs Wartime, Refugee Past," *Jewish News of Northern California*, September 18, 1998, https://jweekly.com/1998/09/18/berkeley-architect-reconstructs-wartime-refugee-past.

181. Levitch, *From Beginning to Beginning*, 59.

182. Ibid.

183. "Former Refugee Returns to Oswego's 'Safe Haven,'" *Oswego Palladium-Times*, May 25, 1993.

184. Lowenstein, *Token Refuge*, 192.

185. "Refugee Student Winner of First Prize in Contest," *Oswego Palladium-Times*, January 8, 1946, 2.

186. Gruber, *Haven*, 231.

187. "Former Refugee Returns," *Oswego Palladium-Times*.

188. Smith, "Influence of Ralph M. Faust," 31.

189. Warnes, Hill, Fisher, Kahl, Coe-Rappaport, *Don't Fence Me In*, 37.

190. Winters papers, Special Collections, Penfield Library, SUNY Oswego.

191. Levitch, *From Beginning to Beginning*, 58–59.

192. Gruber, *Haven*, 182.

193. Paul Bokros obituary, *Boothbay Register*, April 26, 2021, https://www.boothbayregister.com/article/paul-bokros/146189.

194. Harris, "Berkeley Architect Reconstructs Wartime."

195. Warnes, Hill, Fisher, Kahl, Coe-Rappaport, *Don't Fence Me In*, 69.

196. Lowenstein, *Token Refuge*, 169.

197. Winters papers, Special Collections, Penfield Library, SUNY Oswego.

198. Matthew Reitz, "Safe Haven Honors 2 For Humanitarian Efforts," *Fulton Valley News*, June 26, 2017.

199. "Safe Haven Museum Formally Dedicated," *Oswego Palladium-Times*, October 7, 2002, 2A.

Chapter 9

200. Marks, Krug and Myer, *Token Shipment*, 20–21.

201. Warnes, Hill, Fisher, Kahl, Coe-Rappaport, *Don't Fence Me In*, 6.

202. Muriel Perry oral interview, July 1, 2001, oral history 274, Special Collections, Penfield Library, SUNY Oswego.

203. "Taken for Granted, U.S. Freedoms," reminiscences of Muriel A. Perry, Oswego Public Library, Oswego, NY, Safe Haven digital collection.

204. Perry interview.

205. Frances Marion Brown, Safe Haven 50th reunion interviews, 1994, Penfield Library Archives, SUNY Oswego.

206. "Taken for Granted, U.S. Freedoms."

207. Perry interview.

208. Finkelstein, *Shelter and the Fence*, 89.

209. Brown, Safe Haven 50th reunion interviews.

210. Perry interview.

211. "Taken for Granted, U.S. Freedoms."

212. "Shop Courses at Refugee Shelter Start Next Week," *Oswego Palladium-Times*, November 25, 1944, 15.

213. Thomas Crabtree, "Industrial Training Department," *Ontario Chronicle*, April 26, 1945, 3.

214. Warnes, Hill, Fisher, Kahl, Coe-Rappaport, *Don't Fence Me In*, 51.

215. "Frank Barbeau Photographer and Wizard," *Ontario Chronicle*, May 24, 1945, 2.
216. Brown, Safe Haven 50th reunion interviews.
217. "Student's Tribute to Muriel Perry," *Oswego County Messenger*, June 22, 1981, 6.

Chapter 10

218. "Mrs. Roosevelt Visits Refugee Center," *Oswego Palladium-Times*, September 20, 1944, 14.
219. "Mrs. Roosevelt Delighted with Refugee Center," *Oswego Palladium-Times*, September 21, 1944, 18.
220. "Former Safe Haven Refugee Tells True Tale of the Times," *Oswego Palladium-Times*, September 2002.
221. Ibid.
222. David Levy and Zdenka Ruchwarger Levy oral interview, August 6, 1994, U.S. Holocaust Memorial Museum Collection, acquired from Safe Haven Inc.
223. "Refugee Tells True Tale," *Oswego Palladium-Times*.
224. Levy and Levy interview.
225. Gabriel Greschler, Zdenka's Story of WWII Survival in Croatia and Italy: 'Others Had It Worse,'" *Jewish News of Northern California*, March 10, 2020, https://jweekly.com/2020/03/10/palo-alto-womans-story-of-wwii-survival-in-croatia-and-italy-others-had-it-worse/.
226. Lowenstein, *Token Refuge*, 180, 186.
227. Dr. Salisbury oral interview, November 1983.
228. "Hold Second of Shelter Forums Tuesday Evening," *Oswego Palladium-Times*, October 30, 1944, 9.
229. "German Citizens Love Hitler for Restoring Faith," *Oswego Palladium-Times*, November 28, 1938, 5.
230. "Miss Mahar, 25 Years on OSTC Faculty, Dies," *Oswego Palladium-Times*, February 11, 1960, 4.
231. Warnes, Hill, Fisher, Kahl, Coe-Rappaport, *Don't Fence Me In*, 73.
232. Aulus Saunders oral interview, 1984, oral history 279, Special Collections, Penfield Library, SUNY Oswego.
233. "Gives Doll to Refugee," *Oswego Palladium-Times*, August 7, 1944, 4.
234. Saunders interview.
235. Warnes, Hill, Fisher, Kahl, Coe-Rappaport, *Don't Fence Me In*, 27–28.

236. Finkelstein, *Shelter and the Fence*, 108–9.

237. "Investigation of Problems Presented by Refugees at Fort Ontario Refugee Shelter," 55.

238. A.J. Desmond and Son, "Rajko Ralph Margulis, M.D.," https://www.desmondfuneralhome.com/obituaries/Rajko-Ralph-Margulis-MD?obId=12338820.

239. UCSF Department of Radiology and Biomedical Imaging, "Alexander R. Margulis, M.D.," https://radiology.ucsf.edu/blog/alexander-r-margulis-md-1921-2018.

240. Gruber, *Haven*, 256, 258.

241. Saunders interview.

Chapter 11

242. "Scout Troop of Refugees Will Be Formed," *Oswego Palladium-Times*, September 28, 1944, 7.

243. "Sons of Shelter Residents Start Troop of Scouts," *Oswego Palladium-Times*, December 18, 1945, 8.

244. Harold Clark oral interview, oral history 278, Harold Clark Special Collections, Penfield Library, SUNY Oswego.

245. Letter from Mike Nussbaum, Harold Clark Collection, Special Collections, Penfield Library, SUNY Oswego, SH 5.

246. Greenberg interview.

247. Harold Clark oral interview, oral history 278, Special Collections, Penfield Library, SUNY Oswego.

248. Lowenstein, *Token Refuge*, 146.

249. Gruber, *Haven*, 232–33.

250. Kristen Graham, "These Siblings Fled the Holocaust for the U.S. Almost 80 Years Ago. The War in Ukraine Hits Home," *Philadelphia Enquirer*, March 26, 2022, Holocaust Awareness Museum.

251. Mona Lisa Gioconda oral history interview, United States Holocaust Memorial Museum Collection, acquired from Safe Haven Inc.

252. "Six New Troops in Oswego Area of Girl Scouts," *Oswego Palladium-Times*, January–December 1945.

253. Gruber, *Haven*, 232–33.

254. Ibid., 233.

255. "Girl Scouts at Shelter Invested," *Oswego Palladium-Times*, January 11, 1946, 4.

256. Sylvain Boni remembrances, Special Collections, Penfield Library, SUNY Oswego, SH 11.

257. Robert Peterson, ed., "Scouting in a World War II Refugee Troop," *Scouting Magazine*, November–December 1999, scoutingmagazine.org/issues/0410/d-wwas.html.

258. "Investigation of Problems Presented by Refugees at Fort Ontario Refugee Shelter," 24–30.

259. Moric Kahmi letter, Harold Clark Collection, Special Collections, Penfield Library, SUNY Oswego, SH 5.

260. "Troop 19 Only Unit in State Working with Migrant Scouts," *Oswego Palladium-Times*, July 28, 1959.

261. Clark interview.

262. Geni, "Prof. Mirko Nussbaum," https://www.geni.com/people/Prof-Mirko-Nussbaum/6000000087552712854.

263. Greenberg interview.

264. "One of the Scouting Veterans," *Oswego County Messenger*, February 5, 1982, 9.

265. "Harold D. Clark, Minetto Historian, Scouting Enthusiast," *Oswego Valley News*, November 27, 1989.

266. Lavinia Edmunds, "Recyclables Have Special Booster on Capitol Hill," *Washington Post*, June 25, 1981; "Esther Morrison, Professor and Recycling Activist, Dies," *Washington Post*, September 24, 1989.

Chapter 12

267. "Refugees Guests of Young Women," *Oswego Palladium-Times*, September 25, 1944, 5.

268. "Refugee Shelter Director Speaks," *Oswego Palladium-Times*, October 14, 1944.

269. "Refugee Tells Rotarians How He Fled Nazis," *Oswego Palladium-Times*, October 21, 1944, 10.

270. "Former Yugoslav Scout Speaks to Pontiac Leaders," *Oswego Palladium-Times*, October 30, 1944, 12.

271. "Permit Granted for Refugees to Assist Farmers," *Oswego Palladium-Times*, September 21, 1944, 4.

272. "250 Refugees at Fort Willing to Assist Farmers," *Oswego Palladium-Times*, September 25, 1944, 10.

273. Naomi Jolles, "Oswego's Children Adopt Little Refugees," *New York Post*, November 22, 1944, 8.

274. "Refugee Center Seeks Hospital Facilities Here," *Oswego Palladium-Times*, November 27, 1944.

275. "Chanukah Festival in the Shelter," *Ontario Chronicle*, December 1944.

276. "Center Seeks Hospital Facilities," *Oswego Palladium-Times*.

277. "No Substitute for Toys?: What People Say," *Oswego Palladium-Times*, December 27, 1944, 8.

278. "National Radio Broadcast," *Ontario Chronicle*, December 28, 1944, 1.

279. "Safe Haven," *Oswego Palladium-Times*, July 26, 2004, 3A.

280. Miss Wood Collection, Special Collections, Penfield Library, SUNY Oswego, SH-4 (Part 2).

281. Gruber, *Haven*, 197–98.

282. Ibid.

283. Baron, *Haven from the Holocaust*, 28.

284. "Refugees Will Buy War Bonds," *Oswego Palladium-Times*, January 1945.

285. "Refugee Killed When Coal Pile Collapses," *Oswego Palladium-Times*, February 24, 1945, 7.

286. Eleanor Morehead, "Refugees at Oswego Want to Go to the U.S.A.," *New York Post*, March 19, 1945, 12.

287. "What to Do Baffles Fort Ontario Refugees," *New York Post*, March 19, 1945, 8.

288. "Refugee Student Has Praise for Bill of Rights," *Oswego Palladium-Times*, February 22, 1945, 11.

289. "Three Telegrams," *Ontario Chronicle*, April 19, 1945, 3, Special Collections, Penfield Library, SUNY Oswego.

290. Joseph Smart oral history interview.

291. "Friends of Fort Ontario Guest—Refugees: A Statement by the Sponsors Committee," Special Collections, Penfield Library, SUNY Oswego.

292. Oswego County Historical Society, "Closing the Emergency Refugee Shelter at Fort Ontario," https://www.rbhousemuseum.org/wp-content/uploads/2018/05/ClosingShelterSM.pdf.

Chapter 13

293. "Large Majority at Shelter Want to Remain Here," *Oswego Palladium-Times*, May 16, 1945, 14.

294. "Statement about the Situation of the Refugees at Fort Ontario: What People Say," *Oswego Palladium-Times*, May 26, 1945, 4.

295. "What People Say," *Oswego Palladium-Times*, May 29, 1945, 3.

296. Ibid., 5.

297. "What People Say," *Oswego Palladium-Times*, June 4, 1945, 6.

298. "What People Say," *Oswego Palladium-Times*, June 23, 1945, 3.

299. "Let's Clarify Status of These Refugees," *Syracuse Herald Journal*, June 25, 1945, 10.

300. "Investigation of Problems Presented by Refugees at Fort Ontario Refugee Shelter," 53–72.

301. Ibid., 89.

302. Susan Keeter, "A Ship, a Fort and the Medical School Meeting," Upstate University Hospital, June 19, 2014, https://www.upstate.edu/whatsup/2014/0619-a-ship-a-fort-and-the-medical-school-meeting.php.

303. "Investigation of Problems Presented by Refugees at Fort Ontario Refugee Shelter," 89.

304. Ibid., 90–195.

305. "Scholastic Work Done by Refugees," *Oswego Palladium-Times*, June 26, 1945, 10.

306. Gruber, *Haven*, 228–29.

307. "What People Say," *Oswego Palladium-Times*, July 23, 1945, 3.

308. "What People Say," *Oswego Palladium-Times*, July 26, 1945, 3.

309. "What People Say," *Oswego Palladium-Times*, July 27, 1945, 3.

310. "What People Say," *Oswego Palladium-Times*, July 28, 1945, 6.

311. "What People Say," *Oswego Palladium-Times*, July 30, 1945, 3.

312. "What People Say," *Oswego Palladium-Times*, August 4, 1945, 7.

313. "What People Say," *Oswego Palladium-Times*, August 8, 1945, 7.

Chapter 14

314. "Musical Life in the Shelter by Charles Abeles," *Ontario Chronicle*, December 1945; Warnes, Hill, Fisher, Kahl, Coe-Rappaport, *Don't Fence Me In*, 45.

315. Peter Koppitz, "Charles Abele's Survival in Italy," David, https://davidkultur.at/artikel/charles-abeles-ueberleben-in-italien.

316. Marks, Krug and Myer, *Token Shipment*, 100–2.

317. "Present Prizes to Winners of Essay Contest," *Oswego Palladium-Times*, February 17, 1945, 4.

318. "Await Details of Method for Refugee Entry," *Oswego Palladium-Times*, December 24, 1945, 5.

319. Oswego Opera Theater, program insert, November 2022.

320. Eva Kaufman Dye interview transcript, August 6, 1994, Safe Haven Museum.

321. "Kaufman Studio to Open Monday," *Oswego Palladium-Times*, September 14, 1946, 4.

322. "What People Say," *Oswego Palladium-Times*, October 1, 1952,

323. "John B. Kaufman," *Oswego Palladium-Times*, December 3, 1946, 8.

324. Jane Zaia, Safe Haven 50th Reunion Interviews, 1994, Penfield Library Archives, SUNY Oswego.

325. Betsy Zaia Dorman, phone interview, June 11, 2023.

326. "Kaufman Family Soon to Depart for California," *Oswego Palladium-Times*, July 20, 1955, 5.

327. Dye interview.

Chapter 15

328. "Serial Numbers Being Assigned to Registrants," *Oswego Palladium-Times*, March 10, 1942, 10.

329. "Army Calls 20 Volunteers to Begin Training for Wings," *Syracuse Herald Journal*, August 25, 1942, 1.

330. "Oswego Tailor Soon to Leave for West Coast," *Oswego Palladium-Times*, June 8, 1955, 18.

331. Ronald Spereno interview, February 2023.

332. Ibid.

333. Ibid.

334. Oswego High School Yearbook, 1941.

335. Spereno interview.

336. "Tailor Soon to Leave," *Oswego Palladium-Times*, 16.

337. "Fort Ontario Emergency Refugee Shelter," report, Internal Security Department, November 21, 1944, Safe Haven Holocaust Refugee Museum.

338. "J. Kosoff Tailor Shop Taken Over by J. Sylber," advertisement, *Oswego Palladium-Times*, April 22, 1947, 4.
339. Spereno interview.
340. Zaia, Safe Haven 50th Reunion Interviews.
341. "Tailor Soon to Leave," *Oswego Palladium-Times*, 16.
342. Spereno interview;
343. "Escaped Nazi Gas Chambers," *Press-Courier* (Oxnard, CA), 3.
344. Keith Sylber interview, March 23, 2023.
345. "Ventura County Men in Service," *Press-Courier* (Oxnard, CA), June 25, 1969, ancestry.com.
346. "Dr. Albert Sylber," *Park City Daily News* (Bowling Green, KY), December 14, 1990, 10m.

Epilogue

347. Rosenbaum, *No Room for Democracy*, 21–27, 32.
348. Gruber, *Haven*, 176.
349. "Oswego Holocaust Recalled in Albany," *Post Standard*, January 23, 1986, B-4.
350. Lowenstein, *Token Refuge*, 176.
351. Richard Rosenbaum letter to Safe Haven Museum, July 8, 2016.
352. Rosenbaum, *No Room for Democracy*, 33.
353. "Richard Rosenbaum, Former State Supreme Court Justice, Dies," *Democrat and Chronicle*, July 29, 2019, https://www.democratandchronicle.com/story/news/2019/07/29/richard-rosenbaum-former-new-york-state-supreme-court-justice-dies-penfield-ny/1847649001/.
354. Ibid.
355. Joe Klein, "The Last Liberal," *New York*, April 3, 1989, 14.
356. Celeste Katz, "Ray Harding, Powerbroker and Former State Liberal Party Leader, Dead at 77," *New York Daily News*, August 9, 2012.
357. "Antisemitic Vandalism. The word 'Jewish' on the granite refugee shelter memorial was defaced soon after its dedication in 1981. Refugees, Jewish organizations, and others responsible for erecting the memorial met soon afterwards and recommended that the damage remain as a testimony to the continuing presence of antisemitism in society and the need to be vigilant and fight against it." Signage at the monument that still stands at Fort Ontario.
358. Warnes, Hill, Fisher, Kahl, Coe-Rappaport, *Don't Fence Me In*, 71.

359. Rosenbaum letter to Safe Haven Museum.
360. Koppitz, "Abele's Survival."
361. Tyler Theater, program of *The Golden Cage Operetta* production, November 12 and November 13, 2022, SUNY Oswego.

Conclusion

362. Greenberg interview.
363. Ernest Braun letter to Judge George Penney, July 11, 1945, United States Holocaust Memorial Museum.

SELECTED BIBLIOGRAPHY

Baron, Lawrence. *Haven from the Holocaust: Oswego, New York 1944–1946*. Cooperstown: New York History, January 1, 1983.

Cost, Elaine G. *Essays*. Rochester, NY: Fossil Press, 2015.

Finkelstein, Norman. *The Shelter and the Fence*. Chicago, IL: Chicago Review Press, 2021.

Gruber, Ruth. *Haven: The Dramatic Story of 1000 World War II Refugees and How They Came to America*. First printed 1983. Reprint 1984. Reprint, New York: Three Rivers Press, 2000.

"Investigation of Problems Presented by Refugees at Fort Ontario Refugee Shelter." Hearings before the Committee on Immigration and Naturalization, House of Representatives. June 25 and 26, 1945.

Levitch, Edward. *From Beginning to Beginning: An Autobiography*. Berkeley, CA: Mad Dog Publishing Company, 1997.

Lowenstein, Sharon. *Token Refuge: The Story of the Jewish Refugee Shelter at Oswego*. Bloomington: Indiana University Press, 1986.

Marks, Edward B., program officer, War Relocation Authority, U.S. Department of the Interior; J.A. Krug, secretary, War Relocation Authority; and D.S. Myer, director, War Relocation Authority. *Token Shipment: The Story of America's Refugee Shelter*. Rev. ed. by Rebecca J. Fisher and Paul A. Lear. Washington, D.C.: U.S. Government Printing Office, 1946.

Rogers, Dorothy. *Oswego: Fountainhead of Teacher Education*. New York: Appleton-Century Crofts Inc., 1961.

Rosenbaum, Richard M. *No Room for Democracy: The Triumph of Ego over Common Sense*. Rochester, NY: RIT Press, 2008.

Smith, Debra J. Cunningham. "The Influence of Ralph M. Faust." Master's thesis, Department of Curriculum and Instruction, School of Education, State University of New York College at Oswego, July 1996.

Warnes, K., Kevin Hill, Rebecca J. Fisher, Elizabeth Kahl and Judy Coe-Rappaport. *Don't Fence Me In: Memories of the Fort Ontario Refugees and Their Friends*. 2nd ed. Oswego, NY: Safe Haven Museum and Education Center, July 2004.

Wyman, David S. *The Abandonment of the Jews, America and the Holocaust, 1941–1945*. New York: New Press, 1984, 2007.

INDEX

About the Author

After a professional career as a news reporter, editor and college professor, Ann Callaghan Allen retired from teaching in the Department of Communication and Film Studies at Le Moyne College in Syracuse, New York. She returned to her hometown of Oswego, New York, and wrote her first book, *The Madame's Business*, chronicling the life of Malvina Guimaraes, an early entrepreneur who challenged the social norms of her day and built a financial empire, only to see it threatened by an unscrupulous husband who had nineteenth-century law and conventional thinking about a woman's place on his side.